D0946532

STRAND PRICE
$ 5.00

ORANGE COUNTY

"Partners in Progress" by Cynthia Simone
Introduction by Lucien D. Truhill

Produced in Cooperation with the
Orange County Chamber of Commerce

Windsor Publications, Inc.
Northridge, California

ORANGE COUNTY

an economic a celebration

JANET E. GRAEBNER

Windsor Publications, Inc.—History Book Division
Editorial Director: Teri Davis Greenberg
Corporate Biographies Director: Karen Story
Design Director: Alexander D'Anca

Staff for *Orange County*
Editors: Lane Powell, Susan L. Wells
Photo Editor: Laura Cordova
Assistant Photo Editor: Cameron Cox
Assistant Director, Corporate Biographies: Phyllis Gray
Editor, Corporate Biographies: Judith Hunter
Production Editor, Corporate Biographies: Una FitzSimons
Editorial Assistants: Didier Beauvoir, Brenda Berryhill, Thelma Fleischer, Kim Kievman, Kathy B. Peyser, Pam Pittman, Theresa Solis
Sales Representatives: Richard Anstead, Will Lee, Leslie West
Layout Artist, Corporate Biographies: Mari Catherine Preimesberger
Designer: Ellen Ifrah

Library of Congress Cataloging-in-Publication Data

Graebner, Janet E., 1937-

Orange County, an economic celebration/Janet E. Graebner;

"Partners in progress" by Cynthia Simone; introduction by Lucien D. Truhill; produced in cooperation with the Orange County Chamber of Commerce.

—1st ed.

p. cm.

Bibliography p.

Includes index.

ISBN 0-89781-243-3

1. Orange County (Calif.)—History. 2. Orange County (Calif.)—Description and travel—Views. 3. Orange County (Calif.)—Industries. I. Simone, Cynthia. II. Orange County Chamber of Commerce (Calif.) III. Title.

F869.O6G73 1988   88-85

979.4'96—dc 19   CIP

©1988 by Windsor Publications, Inc.
All Rights Reserved
Published 1988
Printed in the United States of America
First Edition
Windsor Publications, Inc.

Elliot Martin, Chairman of the Board
James L. Fish III, Chief Operating Officer
Hal Silverman, Vice-President/Publisher

FRONTISPIECE: The last moments of twilight glitter at Dana Point Harbor. Photo by Mark E. Gibson

FACING PAGE: Umbrellas are a bright counterpoint along rainy Santa Ana streets. Photo by Jim Mendenhall

DUST COVER: Orange County Performing Arts Center, in Costa Mesa. Photo by Yana Bridle

To the founders, sponsors, and participants of
Orange County Centennial, Inc.,
and to Orange Countians, who have made the
region a place worth celebrating

CONTENTS

People with a strong entrepreneurial sense abound in Orange County. Working in relative harmony, they maintain an economy of national and international influence.

Besides sun, surf, and sand, the region's cultural, educational, and religious opportunities combine to make Orange County ideal for the 'whole' man or woman.

Orange County is a microcosm of California's economic influence, and a model for the next century of American business.

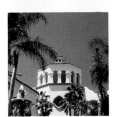

PREFACE

Change is such an integral part of Orange County's history that attempts to capture "the moment" are quickly superseded by new moments. During the course of researching and writing *Orange County: An Economic Celebration*, new companies formed, some failed, executive positions changed, more construction took place, plans got underway for the county's centennial celebration, and a twenty-seventh city, Mission Viejo, was born; circumstances, among others, that necessitate, in a work of this sort, constant revision of the manuscript.

What does that say about Orange County?

That such movement attests to its vitality and strength, and to its innovative attitude that can, after 100 years, still present a unified purpose directed toward its future.

And, on a deeper level, that Orange County is not just its physical accomplishments, but, more important, it is people. Real people with a sense—and sensitivity—of commitment to making Orange County a better place to work and live.

It is this latter quality: commitment, plus a spirit of compromise—often arising from the heat of controversy—that characterizes Orange Countians, and that outsiders (especially national publications writing about the county) fail to understand.

This book has been written, in part, to reveal that spirit, that Orange County psyche. It is not meant to be a chronological narrative of Orange County's economic history, but instead to show some broad concepts lying behind its growth, especially during the last quarter century, and to present some insights into what Orange Countians envision for the next century.

My experience while writing this book was one of immense pleasure, and I thank Lucien Truhill, Beverly Cearley, and Anson McArthur of the Orange County Chamber of Commerce for recommending me for the project; Martin Brower for his generous sharing of ideas; Susan Wells and Lane Powell, of Windsor Publications, for their editorial guidance; and Orange Countians, who are the real writers of Orange County's economic celebration.

PREVIOUS PAGE: Beachgoers enjoy the last glowing rays of the sun at Corona del Mar. Photo by John Sanford

FACING PAGE: Dynamic buildings distinguish Santa Ana's Hutton Centre. Photo by Jim Mendenhall

A MODEL FOR AMERICAN ENTERPRISE

A dramatic stretch of coast is seen in this photo by Jeff Marks

INTRODUCTION

Starting with the founding of Mission San Juan Capistrano by Father Junipero Serra in the year 1776, Orange County has woven a colorful and proud historical tapestry.

The area soon evolved from the early mission governance into that of the Spanish land grants, thus fostering the birth of the great rancheros, remnants of which, even today, play a part in Orange County's land development.

With the coming of the settlers after the American Civil War, the creation of new towns like Anaheim, Orange, and Santa Ana commenced.

By August 1889 the establishment of the county as an official arm of government announced the beginning of a new era; one characterized by deep roots planted firmly in a powerful emerging economy: the citrus industry. The industry—symbolized by the well-known Valencia orange—helped the county to successfully make the economic transition into the twentieth century.

During the first three decades of the century—which saw the development of a physical infrastructure and a network of roads and railways that were quite outstanding for the time—Orange County's growth as an agricultural and horticultural region was largely governed by a wealthy and educated citrus growers aristocracy, thus earning it the name, the "Orange Empire."

Then World War I and the Great Depression brought changes to the county's social and economic structure. Cities like Anaheim, Santa Ana, and Fullerton began campaigns to attract industry in order to increase employment opportunities for their growing populations.

Agriculture, however, continued to hold on to its economic importance. As late as 1953, the chamber (working under its original name, the Associated Chambers of Orange County) was still proclaiming in its "Majestic Empire" brochure that the county was one of the ten wealthiest agricultural areas in the United States.

In 1955, the same year Disneyland opened, the first of the freeways extending out of Los Angeles entered the county, and the rush for land was on: for industry, for commerce, and for housing. It is a rush that has slowed down in recent years but has truly never stopped!

Lured by exceptional employment opportunities and a favorable entrepreneurial climate, Orange County has changed dramatically during the last 33 years from an economically strong agricultural community to an economically strong world-class, sophisticated, urban metropolis.

Orange County now ranks tenth among all metro markets in the United States, exceeding 23 of the states and such regional markets as Atlanta, Dallas, St. Louis, Pittsburgh, and San Francisco.

In California, we are succeeded only by the Los Angeles Metro Area; and were we a nation, our gross national product would rate fortieth in the world.

Orange County is considered a world-class metro area because of its educational, cultural, scientific, and economic strengths. We have two of the world's top theme parks; our own World Trade Center Association; one of the most heavily booked convention centers in Amer-

Mission Viejo is seen from across the water. Photo by Yana Bridle

ica; a stadium that is home to both a major baseball and football franchise; a repertory theatre and a performing arts center; plus several first-rate art museums, to name only a few of the county's assets.

Linking this coastal haven of enterprise to numerous leisure activities are 42 miles of the most scenic coastline anywhere, which includes two of the fullest small-boat harbors in the world: Newport Beach and Dana Point.

Orange County: An Economic Celebration is the title of this book. First of all, it is a celebration of 76 years of service for the Orange County Chamber of Commerce, an organization whose mission will certainly change and grow with the times just as it has since its founding in 1912.

Second, the book celebrates Orange County's centennial. Beginning in August 1988, Orange Countians will participate in a year-long birthday party that has been organized by Orange County Centennial, Inc., a non-profit organization established by the board of directors of the chamber.

If Orange County is truly (as has been stated by various national reports) a foretaste of the future of America, then the county's business and community leaders must be united in their determination to bring together the social, business, and public infrastructure. We can maintain a progressive, dynamic, and developing economic entity only through the formation of consensus programs designed to solve the problems that face us today.

Many believe and affirm that this county of ours is on the threshold of its greatest years. I agree. And as it has for the past decades of our economic growth, may Orange County continue its position as a leading metropolitan area in helping to guide America toward its future greatness.

Lucien D. Truhill, C.I.D.
President and Chief Executive Officer
Orange County Chamber of Commerce

RIPE FOR ENTERPRISE

WE USED TO MAKE FUN OF ORANGE COUNTY AS FARM-LAND TURNED TO MICKEY MOUSE. NOW WE "TAKE" FUN THERE AND MARVEL AT THE TRANSFORMATION.

—ART SEIDENBAUM,

LOS ANGELES TIMES

With a speed that is nearly impossible to comprehend, Orange County, within the last thirty years, has been transformed from an anonymous agricultural area that caught the overflow populace from Los Angeles County into an urban—and urbane— economic, social, and cultural environment.

Originally exemplifying the suburban "bedroom borough" of the 1950s and 1960s, Orange County today presents a metropolitan mosaic with a diversified economy that resists the traditional classifications so useful to historians and social analysts. No single city or industry dominates. No long-established ruling elite or "old money" has ceded to another power group. No boundaries circumscribe a central district easily identified as Orange County's "downtown" or urban core. When *National Geographic, Time,* and *Christian Science Monitor* covered the area, reporters did not focus on a particular city as the hub of commerce and culture, but instead wrote about *Orange County* as an economic entity. The articles indicated clearly, through the profiles of various cities, what many Orange Countians already knew: The sum of 27 cities and nine unincorporated communities is greater than the parts.

—Anaheim has a toehold on tourism. The world walks through Disneyland's magic portals. Thousands more pass through Anaheim stadium's gates to watch major-league baseball and football with the California Angels or the Los Angeles Rams. Some of the nation's foremost trade shows and conferences book Anaheim Convention Center (the West Coast's largest "showcase," with 685,000 square feet and expanding) years in advance (the scheduling of the International Communica-

FACING PAGE: An orange tree laden with fruit soaks up the sun near Irvine Spectrum. Photo by Yana Bridle

tions Association, which will send 13,000 delegates to Anaheim in June 2001, is an extreme example).

• Santa Ana is the county seat and the home of the World Trade Center Association and John Wayne Airport.

• Buena Park hosts Knott's Berry Farm.

• Cypress sounds the bell daily at Los Alamitos Race Course.

• Costa Mesa claims the nationally known South Coast Plaza and Crystal Court shopping malls, South Coast Repertory Theatre, Pacific Amphitheatre, and the world-class, privately funded Orange County Performing Arts Center.

• Newport Beach is home to Newport Harbor Art Museum and Newport Center's Fashion Island retail emporium.

• Irvine is the site of the Irvine Business Complex and Irvine Spectrum, a commercial research and technology development located on 2,200 acres near the University of California (UCI).

And the list goes on—Westminster, Garden Grove, Orange, Tustin, La Habra, Seal Beach, San Clemente—with each city donating its particular character to the total Orange County psyche.

CITY	INCORPORATED	UNINCORPORATED
Anaheim	1878	Capistrano Beach
Brea	1917	Dana Point
Buena Park	1953	El Toro
Costa Mesa	1953	El Toro Station
Cypress	1956	Laguna Hills
Fountain Valley	1957	Laguna Niguel
Fullerton	1904	Rossmoor
Garden Grove	1956	South Laguna
Huntington Beach	1909	Tustin Foothills
Irvine	1971	
Laguna Beach	1927	
La Habra	1925	
La Palma	1955	
Los Alamitos	1960	
Mission Viejo	1988	
Newport Beach	1906	
Orange	1888	
Placentia	1926	
San Clemente	1928	
San Juan Capistrano	1961	
Santa Ana	1886	
Seal Beach	1915	
Stanton	1956	
Tustin	1927	
Villa Park	1962	
Westminster	1957	
Yorba Linda	1967	

Orange County's "original settlements" have undertaken extensive redevelopment programs, while younger, master-planned communities like Mission Viejo and Rancho Santa Margarita, located in the southern part of the county, offer living environments on the cusp of history as they develop new spatial and social formations to accommodate a swelling population estimated to reach 2.6 million by the year 2000 and 2.8 million by the year 2010.

Forty-two miles of coastline link Laguna Beach arts with Newport

South Coast Plaza remains one of today's most successful shopping malls. Photo by Jeff Marks

New homes await owners at Santa Margarita. Photo by Jim Mendenhall

Beach yachts and Huntington Beach industry, and dozens of commercial centers, industrial parks, hotels, and high-rise office buildings sprout from land that formerly yielded asparagus, lettuce, lima beans, and strawberries.

Where the scent of orange blossoms once perfumed the air, now children's voices waft on the breeze from "groves" of community developments replete with schools and universities, libraries, churches, neighborhood shopping malls, hospitals and research institutions, entertainment and sports complexes, museums and art galleries.

In the central portion of the county, Garden Grove's soaring glass Crystal Cathedral is balanced in the South County by the rotund adobe walls of San Juan Capistrano's Old Mission and New Church.

Just off Costa Mesa's bustling Bristol Street the peaceful atmosphere captured by sculptor Isamu Noguchi's *California Scenario* is repeated at Sherman Library and Gardens in Corona del Mar, a few steps away from the Pacific Coast Highway. Erasing the 1960s picture of Orange County as the hinterland homestead of people migrating from an overcrowded "City of Angels," *Los Angeles Times'* Art Seidenbaum, after a visit to Costa Mesa in 1983, wrote, "We used to make fun of Orange County as farmland turned to Mickey Mouse. Now we *take* fun there and marvel at the transformation."

Never before has one area captured so much in so little time. Flanked on the west by the Pacific Ocean and by Riverside and San Bernardino counties on the east, with Los Angeles 40 miles north and San Diego 90 miles south, Orange County's 786 square miles are neither city nor

ABOVE: Mission San Juan Capistrano stands in the center of town. Photo by Michele Burgess

ABOVE, LEFT: The Crystal Cathedral is the center of a worldwide congregation. Courtesy, Crystal Cathedral

mere suburb. It is its own place, and according to the *Orange County Register*, the second-largest daily in Southern California, Orange County is a "unique metroplex."

Embroidering that phrase, Hank Koehn (founder and late chairman of the Los Angeles-based TRIMTAB Futures Group), while speaking to Orange County's Business Development Association in 1985, was prompted to describe the county as "undergoing the gentle, subtle emergence of a twenty-first-century metroplex. It is a mixed-use place and one with tremendous ethnic vitality; a region inventing itself out of opportunities of the future."

True. And many of these opportunities are weighted in favor of the county's economic diversification: manufacturing and distribution, aerospace and defense electronics, biotechnology and high technology (medical, analytical and scientific instruments, lasers, computers and related products, communications and diagnostic systems, among others).

The county's growth and stability is further enhanced by contributions from non-technical fields: health care, tourism, retail, construction, real estate development, and financial and professional services.

What is left to challenge Orange County's commercial community?

International trade. Still furled, but unfolding rapidly as a strong fix on future opportunities, companies engaged in world commerce or related services already provide 25 percent of the jobs in Orange County.

Both domestic and world trade benefit greatly from the county's location between Los Angeles and San Diego, which allows access to eight

TOP: A hint of sunlight sneaks in at Corona del Mar's Sherman Gardens. Photo by Mark E. Gibson

BOTTOM: Shopping and dining are a pleasure in this sunny plaza. Photo by Jeff Marks

freeways, four rail and three bus lines, four seaports (Long Beach, San Diego, and two in Los Angeles), and five airports (John Wayne-Orange County, Los Angeles International, Long Beach Municipal, Ontario International in Riverside County, and San Diego International). Fullerton Airport and Meadowlark Airport in Huntington Beach service smaller aircraft.

Given its natural attributes: sunshine, surf and sand, Mediterranean climate, the golden promise of a good life—often the initial features that attract people to the area—it is difficult to speak of Orange County without repeating the kind of patter usually reserved for promotional color brochures.

In the absence of a major body of published in-depth research on Orange County's evolution in three decades from rural to urban status,

Dana Point Harbor shelters these novice windsurfers. Photo by Jim Mendenhall

how, then, does one begin to address this rapid transformation? What is the primary force propelling this centennial-bound county, which is expected to outperform both California and the nation in economic growth and employment through the turn of the century?

People. Daring, visionary people with a strong entrepreneurial flair and a can-do mentality. People with a secure sense of place . . . Anchors.

For example, the majority of residents have lived in Orange County for more than 10 years and 68 percent own their homes, according to the 1984 *Orange County Annual Survey*, a study by Mark Baldassare (a professor at the University of California, Irvine) designed to track the economic, demographic, and political trends of California's third- (and the nation's seventh-) most populous county.

Furthermore, Orange Countians are financially comfortable. The median household income in 1986 was $41,000, far surpassing the national median of $22,000. Compared to one in six households claiming a $50,000 income in 1982 (when the first UCI survey was conducted), one in three households earned that amount in 1986.

Anchors: The county is undergoing the development of a native population that is well educated. The U.S. Census Bureau reported 130,760 residents in April 1940 and just over 216,000 in 1950. Kindled by vast amounts of undeveloped land and the budding aerospace and tourism industries, Orange County's population tripled in the 1960s to nearly 704,000, shooting to a 23 percent average annual population growth (compared to the 1950s' 7 percent increase).

A corresponding reduction of in-migration occurred as the county's talented ethnic mix (78.4 percent white, 14.8 percent Hispanic, 4.7 percent Asian and Pacific Island, 2 percent other, according to the 1980 census) settled into a period of refining what the early influx had wrought. A decline in growth commenced during the 1970s (10 percent annually) and continues in the 1980s. The eighties record a modest annual population increase of about 3 percent, with in-migration accounting for only 13 percent.

These rooted residents are schooled. Three-fourths of the nearly 2.2 million population (January 1986 estimate) have at least some college education, and graduates from the two largest formal institutions—UCI (dedicated in 1964) and California State University, Fullerton (CSUF, established in 1959 as Orange County State College)—are prone to remaining here. Since opening their doors, university officials claim that over 75 percent of CSUF's graduates, and approximately 60 percent of UCI's alumni, have accepted employment in the area, thus ensuring a solid base of skilled labor.

The proverbial little red schoolhouse on the corner disappeared long ago as Orange County's educational infrastructure spread in every direction. Four community college districts operate eight campuses. Branches of the University of Southern California, West Coast University, Western State University College of Law, and Pepperdine University complement courses offered at UCI and CSUF. Various vocational, adult education, and regional occupational programs dot the county

LEFT: This elegant Lido Island house features an inviting harborside pool and spa. Photo by Yana Bridle

FACING PAGE: John Wayne Airport connects Orange County with the world. Photo by Jim Mendenhall

from east to west, north to south.

From technical certificates to undergraduate and doctoral degrees, from the liberal arts to optometry to the ministry, from classroom participation to extensive learn-at-home courses beamed via television broadcasts, Orange County could be considered one giant classroom.

The educational institution that started it all? Chapman College, which was founded as a private school in 1861 in northern California. Initially called Hesperian College, then California Christian College, the name was changed in 1934 to Chapman College. The establishment was moved to the City of Orange in 1954, making it the oldest higher-education school in the county. Today, says long-time resident reporter and all-time Orange County booster, Jim Dean, "the college is supported by major industrial institutions in the county [that are] headed by former students who have become successful business leaders" (MG).

Anchors: The business community grows on its own success. Approximately 90 percent of Orange County's estimated 80,000 companies started small and expanded as the years presented opportunities for developing a multi-dimensional economy that keeps over 1.2 million people in jobs. About 75 percent of the employed residents work within the county. It is this capacity for internal growth, observers claim—coupled with the fact that many businesses are in the early stages of their life cycles, and therefore ripe for expansion—that will sustain the county's economy in the future. "We are the leading county in the nation for start-up small businesses," says Susan Lentz, executive director of the World Trade Center Association, "and some of those will be the IBMs of the world."

FACING PAGE: A young business-
man strolls through a plaza. Photo
by Yana Bridle

Entrepreneurism has been at the heart of Orange County's development from the beginning. Historically grounded in the spirited attitude of Spanish missionaries and explorers who arrived in the mid-1700s (documented in *The Golden Promise, An Illustrated History of Orange County,* by San Juan Capistrano historian Pamela Hallan-Gibson), and imbued with a sense of independence similar to that of their forebears, who pushed for and gained jurisdictional autonomy from Los Angeles County in March 1889, contemporary Orange Countians exhibit the same enthusiasm and intensity, a quality much admired by Jewel Plummer Cobb, who in October 1981 became CSUF's third president. "If Orange County were placed in the desert 200 miles east," she says, "it would be complete as an entity; a mature, intact, autonomous county."

Having lived in several states over the years, Cobb has a base for comparing what she calls "the land of fresh-squeezed orange juice" with other locales.

The anchors in Orange County are exceptional. There is a very strong, relatively well-to-do middle class which is contributing in very positive ways to the economic growth and development of the county ... There is no comparison [elsewhere] with the hard work and commitment that I see here, [and] I'm always impressed with a certain strength, straightforwardness, honesty, and openness that emanates from Orange Countians.

A partial explanation, perhaps, for the county's rapid quarter-century transition lies in the fact that this well-educated, financially comfortable middle class is also predominantly middle aged, thus providing leaders at the business, government, social, and political levels who are at the peak of their professional maturity and eager to implement new ideas and rework old ones. (In 1986, the median age in Orange County—meaning half the people were older and half younger—was 28.5 years for males and 30.5 years for females. The median age of all Americans was 31.8 years.)

Certainly this "youthfulness" is what attracted Todd Nicholson, president of the Industrial League of Orange County, who arrived in September 1972—"for a year or two"—and stayed. Although the characters and the details change, it is a story heard often in Orange County.

Specifically, Nicholson recalls, "I came for the opportunity that I saw with what was then the Greater Irvine Industrial League." (Established in 1970 in the City of Irvine, the 800-member organization, representing companies that employ over 126,000 people, changed its name in 1982 to more accurately reflect the membership, geographic spread, and activities involving countywide public policy issues, like surface and airport transportation, financing, and housing.)

Says Nicholson:

One of the things that caught my eye very early on, and that continues to excite me today, is that this is a young community. In a lot of metropolitan centers I think what you tend to see is the old guard; the longtime, older, moneyed people who are holding on to the status quo. I came from a community like that [Tacoma, Washington], where established lumber baron-type families who ran the city didn't like change. New

ideas and concepts and approaches weren't particularly welcome. It's just the opposite in Orange County.

The opposite has catapulted Orange County into the top 40 economies of the *world*, generating a $50 billion gross county product in 1986. Among metropolitan-area rankings it is sixteenth in population (between Pittsburgh, Pennsylvania, and San Diego, California); tenth in buying power; thirteenth in retail sales; and, not surprisingly, a "moneybags" with respect to bank deposits. The 1986 *Chapman College Economic & Business Review* forecast total bank deposits of $17.5 billion for 1987, an increase of 107 percent since 1981. James L. Doti, dean of Chapman College's School of Business and Management and director of the Center for Economic Research, noted that "total deposits in Los Angeles and Orange County banks now rival that of the nation's number-one money center, New York City."

Despite all the cheerleading, there is some trouble in paradise. In the twilight of the twentieth century, residents and city and county officials continue to struggle with the problems of freeway and airport congestion, affordable housing, air pollution, and disposal of toxic wastes. "The problems typify that Orange County has 'arrived' and is a defined community," observes Ronald L. Merriman, managing partner at Peat Marwick's Center Tower offices in Costa Mesa.

For the future, several issues currently dominating discussion at the state and national levels might eventually require closer examination by local government: regulation and taxation of businesses and the question of immigration. "These are matters of particular importance to Orange County's small-business community," says the Industrial League's Nicholson, "but they are of concern, really, to all business."

A subject uppermost in nearly everyone's mind—due largely to clogged surface transportation arteries, which shorten tempers and lengthen travel time—is the possible destruction of the very quality of life that has attracted and motivated Orange Countians for decades. In the latter eighties, the product of this concern is a mounting no-growth versus slow-growth attitude. For the present, the debate is a parry-thrust situation between those who oppose more growth and those who support it. But more deliberate action might be forthcoming if a growth limitation initiative is introduced.

The growth debate is healthy, a *Los Angeles Times* editorial pointed out (2/22/87). Orange Countians cannot put the genie back into the bottle. Growth will continue. Few people disagree on that. The real bone of contention is how much growth, at what rate, and where. The issue will require serious thought on the part of residents—pro and con—as well as city and county governments, because the decisions will definitely influence Orange County's future planning.

"It's a toughy," says Nicholson, who believes that it is balance, rather than no-growth per se, that most people are seeking.

In all the surveys we see, balance is the objective; one that has that lofty goal of maintaining their quality of life and at the same time providing the economic vitality that's necessary for the county. Achieving it is tougher than stating it, but I think that's what we're all after.

The growth debate offers an opportunity for Orange Countians to work

FACING PAGE: These banks gleam of gold in the setting sun. Photo by Jim Mendenhall

together like they never have before, in order to preserve their accomplishments and build—figuratively and literally—for the future. In their inimitable style, they are facing the problems (as we shall see in the following chapters) that were inevitable as the county matured from an agricultural to an urbanized landscape.

Rising to this challenge pinpoints Orange Countians' trademark, the can-do mentality characterizing them from the beginning, which has produced a vibrant economy with a skilled labor force, a higher average wage, a lower unemployment rate, a growing appreciation for the arts and culture, and the myriad other advantages available to imaginative people with a sense of commitment. "There's a feeling of having a piece of the action," states Norm Priest, director of Community Development and Planning for the City of Anaheim.

This is a relatively new urban society. People grew *with Orange County, as opposed to going to a city that had been in place for decades or centuries, like Cincinnati, Detroit or Boston. The aim [for people] in those places was to integrate themselves into the city, whereas in Orange County the people contribute to the growth. I'm reluctant to use a phrase like pioneering spirit, but that's the way I understand it.*

Orange Countians demand more from life than just a job. They also require something to nourish their body, mind, and spirit, the subject of the next chapter. It is this quest for full-circle development, from the physical geography to the inner being, that spells *unique*, a quality that is turning national and international heads—like so many sunflowers seeking the sunshine—towards Orange County, a region ripe for enterprise.

BODY, MIND, AND SPIRIT

IT'S VERY DIFFICULT TO VER-
BALIZE WHY ORANGE COUNTY
IS BETTER THAN ANOTHER
PLACE . . . IT'S 'EYES AND
HEART' TALK.

—JOCK BEGG,
NEWPORT HOME LOAN, INC

Ask someone why he or she lives in a particular city or area and the answers are usually predictable: a company transfer or new job opportunities, good schools, affordable housing, or family ties. Maybe the climate or an attachment to a preferred lifestyle enters the picture.

Probe beyond the tangible reasons and it becomes more difficult, generally, for people to express the whys of where they live. Even in Orange County—sometimes referred to by the media as the culmination of the American Dream, thus easily lending itself to an abundance of superlatives—one may struggle for the words. "It's 'eyes and heart' talk," says Jock Begg, who drives "real slowly" when he and his family return from a trip, "because Orange County is so much a part of us, so relaxing and wonderful."

A co-owner, with Cort Kloke, of Newport Home Loan in Newport Beach, Begg continues: "My reason for being down here is real simple. I grew up in Santa Barbara, where the weather is an edict from God, and this area is the same. My first job out of college was here in Newport Center."

Orange County radiates "a personality, an essence unto itself," Begg adds, "that is just as different as trying to describe individuality in a person."

Words like contribution, loyalty, pride, warmth, energy, fertile ground, self-esteem, and cooperativeness roll from the lips of Orange Countians trying to describe the region in terms that would evoke the reigning spirit—that intrinsic *something*—that has resulted in the county's image of being a good place to live, work, and play.

Indeed, the very phrase *Orange Countian* is significant, expressing

---

FACING PAGE: The sun sets over the San Clemente Pier. Photo by Chris Bryant

A player takes his best shot on one of Laguna Beach's basketball courts. Photo by John Sanford

many residents' sense of belonging to a larger community, one that stretches beyond city borders, exceeding the local distinctions that individual communities project. An Anaheimer, a Santa Anan, a Tustinite, or a Newporter, for example, is also an Orange Countian, a designation that complements one's identification as a member of a particular city.

In the opinion of Anaheim's Norm Priest (Director, Community Development and Planning) the term reflects a reciprocity between people moving in and the county's transition from an agrarian to an urban society, a "mutual growing," he speculates, that took place as new arrivals sought "to plant their feet firmly—maybe they were buying their first home, or starting a new church or business."

In retrospect, Priest suggests that for many it might have been their first time to identify with something and become a part of its development. As a result, the term Orange Countian represents "a unique relationship here that isn't found in most older cities." Says Priest:

There is an Orange County psyche that transcends practical functions, whether business, government, residential, educational, or whatever. There is a loyalty, an attachment . . . I think the neighborhood atmosphere is about the closest I can come to defining Orange County, and that leads to old-fashioned words like neighborliness and cooperation.

Acknowledging Orange County's special amorphous quality, but taking a more pragmatic view, Peat Marwick's Merriman proposes that the question we are struggling to answer is, What sets Orange County apart from major cities with successful economies?

New housing developments characterize areas like Lake Forest, left, and Huntington Beach, right. Photos by Mark E. Gibson

Merriman's reply: "It's a *living economy.* I live where I work and work where I live."

Such was not the case when he lived in Washington, D.C., or Los Angeles. As a long-distance commuter in both cities he experienced little overlap between his family and social life and professional environment. Says Merriman:

In Orange County I don't have to sacrifice what I think is important, or what the individuals in my family want from a home, lifestyle, and support system. If you look at Chicago, Los Angeles, Washington, D.C., or New York, they're basically commuter economies. People go to their jobs, then withdraw from that central business core at the end of the day . . . Sure, we have transportation problems in Orange County, and we're spread out, but I still very much have the sense that I live in my business community.

Merriman is involved in several community organizations, and was involved in preparations for Orange County's year-long centennial cele-

bration, which begins on August 1, 1988. "Orange County owes itself one fine birthday party," he says, "and we want to share it with the rest of the nation, maybe the world. We've got some fairly ambitious plans to do that."

In Merriman's "living economy" his participation in community activities affords an experience he has never had before, which he claims is made more pleasant by the fact that "everybody seems eager to learn from somebody else."

Being involved and willing to learn from others could well stand as Orange County's motto over the years, "while we were putting our dreams into formation and watching them become realities," states Larry Alpert, entrepreneur and sporting goods distributor (Alpert & Associates, Anaheim).

Establishing a well-oiled, diversified economy has been a full-time job in Orange County for more than a quarter century, but the county is more than an economic phenomenon. It is coming full circle and maturing as a social and cultural entity as well.

Balancing their professional and commercial endeavors against personal development and a desire to "make a difference," as one community volunteer remarked, is as characteristic of Orange Countians as the entrepreneurial spirit that shapes the economy.

Through the cultivation and support of the performing arts, educational institutions, art galleries and museums, community work, and other civic affiliations, Orange Countians demonstrate an understanding of, and an appreciation for, the valuable interplay between commercial ambitions and the development of the *total person*.

Let us look briefly at some of these balancers, which absorb the time and energy of the people of the County of Orange, and which could, appropriately, be called nourishment for the body, mind, and spirit.

* * *

"All the way across the country from Broadway, South Coast Repertory Company in Costa Mesa, California, exists as a major force in American drama" (*Horizon*, January/February 1987).

ABOVE: A couple enjoys the last moments of sunshine at the beach. Photo by Jeff Marks

ABOVE, LEFT: Kids express themselves on the walls of the Air House during Music on the Green at the South Coast Metro Center. Photo by John Sanford

FACING PAGE: This boat takes in a day of sunshine at the Woodbridge housing tract in Irvine. Photo by Michele Burgess

Indeed. Orange County's professional resident theater (referred to locally as South Coast Rep or SCR) shines for staging plays that address compelling personal and social issues "in a way that is theatrically exciting and entertaining," says co-founder David Emmes. SCR is also well-known for its regular support of new playwrights, so theatergoers can expect premiere announcements with each season's program.

Moreover, the theater provides a training ground for young actors, and serves as a proving ground for men and women from other walks of life, who view SCR's evening conservatory acting classes as a means of personal growth.

Under the artistic direction of co-founders Emmes and Martin Benson, who in 1963 were operating from the back of a station wagon, SCR's first home was a converted store called Second Step Theatre, located on Newport Boulevard in Costa Mesa.

Arts patrons were convinced that SCR needed space to grow, and since 1978, following what was then the most successful arts funding campaign to date, SCR has been permanently ensconced in its own specifically designed theater complex.

Five acres of land were donated by Costa Mesa developer C.J. Segerstrom & Sons, in that company's South Coast Plaza/Town Center project on Bristol Street. SCR has expanded, both physically and artistically, with the construction of an Artists Center and plans for a second theater. With respect to its programs, SCR continues to influence American theater. In fact, it is considered by some as *the* catalyst for overall improvement of the performing arts in Orange County.

Commenting in 1985 on the county as a cultural wasteland when she had arrived 20 years earlier, former Texan Kathryn Thompson, president and chief executive officer of A & C Properties and Gore Development Corporation, said:

Coming from Dallas, where there were such tremendous cultural opportunities, this was rather a stagnant area by comparison. Then South Coast Repertory planted the seed for cultural development in Orange County. Over the last 20 years it blossomed and grew, and as a result the Orange County Performing Arts [Center] expanded on that. I'm sure it will be internationally known as one of the great theatres of the world (The Executive, *April 1985*).

Confirming the idea that South Coast Repertory Theatre was the "nucleus of what would become a great cultural performing arts center," Henry T. Segerstrom, managing partner for C.J. Segerstrom & Sons, added that it was due to SCR's success in its Town Center location that convinced The Center's board of directors to approve the adjoining site for construction of the performing arts complex that would crown Orange County's cultural achievements.

Probably the most monumental—certainly the most visible—example of Orange Countians' working together to realize a dream was the completion of the privately funded $73 million Orange County Performing Arts Center. Its imposing 120-foot entrance, with sculptor Richard Lippold's *Fire Bird* winging through the inner upper floors and extending outward, dominates the neighboring South Coast Repertory Theatre.

Challenged by Zubin Mehta to "build the proper setting for their music" (following a performance by the Los Angeles Philharmonic in a local high school auditorium), enthusiastic arts supporters laid the groundwork for what would become the Orange County Performing Arts Center, a 3,000-seat facility suitable for staging symphony, ballet, musical theater, and opera.

The Segerstrom family happily donated another five acres (currently valued at over $5 million) plus a gift of $6 million towards the building of a world-class legacy of private enterprise. Nearly 5,000 volunteers, including members from six youth organizations, spent more than 170,000 hours raising construction funds over a three-year period.

Opening night: September 29, 1986, a spectacular gala with medieval-costumed pages stationed on the second-floor balcony to trumpet the arrival of theatergoers. Klieg lights competed with the evening stars and the gilt and gold of elegantly dressed men and women alighting from limousines and exotic cars.

Amidst flowing champagne, guests, natural exuberance, and congratulatory speeches and telegrams, the evening's performance in the main theater, Segerstrom Hall, featured Orange County's Pacific Chorale, under the direction of John Alexander; the Master Chorale of Orange

FACING PAGE: The South Coast Repertory Theatre presents the finest in classic and contemporary drama. Courtesy, South Coast Repertory Theatre

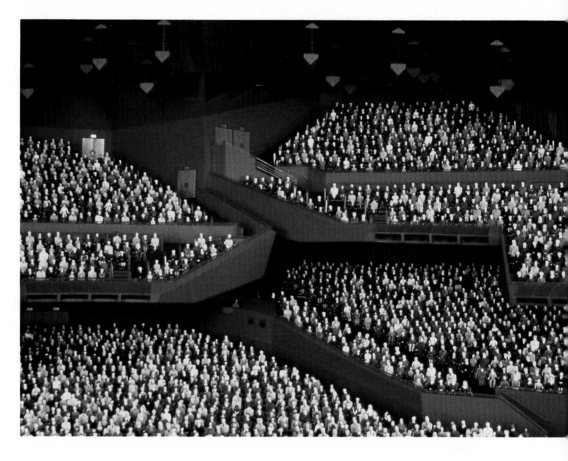

ABOVE: John Driver and Mary Beth Fisher are seen here in the South Coast Repertory Theatre's production of Chekov's *The Seagull*. Courtesy, South Coast Repertory Theatre

ABOVE, RIGHT: The assymetrical seating arrangement in Segerstrom Hall creates intimacy between audience and performer. Courtesy, South Coast Metro

FACING PAGE: Richard Lippold's "Fire Bird" sculpture welcomes visitors to the 3,000 seat Orange County Performing Arts Center. Photo by Jeff Marks

County, directed by Dr. Maurice Allard; and the man who started it all, Zubin Mehta, once again conducting the Los Angeles Philharmonic, in a "proper setting."

Endorsement of The Center's artistic and architectural excellence came during a visit from Beverly Sills, former opera diva and current general director of the New York City Opera, who said: "It's a knockout, a jewel in the crown, [and] I think Los Angeles [home of the L.A. Music Center/Dorothy Chandler Pavilion] is going to have to sit up and pay attention."

Another performing arts triumph followed a decision in March 1987, made by the county's district school board, which approved the construction of the Orange County High School of the Performing Arts. News of the long-awaited facility's reality spread like an open-casting call on Broadway after students at Los Alamitos High School, the site of the new center, heard that final approval had been given for the project.

Los Alamitos High was selected because it has a strong curriculum of visual and performing arts programs. Modeled after the New York High School for the Performing Arts, the Los Alamitos school-within-a-school provides training for promising high school students from Orange County and neighboring Long Beach. Graduates earn a performing arts certificate along with their high school diploma. The Orange County High School of the Performing Arts is the first of its kind in the county and the sixth specialized performing arts school in California.

Two other youth-oriented theater programs are: the Fountain Valley-based Orange County Children's Theatre and the Greater Los Angeles Children's Theatre in Huntington Beach.

RIGHT: Fine art lines the walls at the Susan Spiritus Gallery in South Coast Plaza. Photo by Yana Bridle

FACING PAGE: Contemporary sculptures and paintings are housed at Laguna Beach Art Museum. Photo by Yana Bridle

The possibility that there might be an arts boom in Orange County was suggested in December 1986 by the *Los Angeles Times* in the first of a series of "occasional articles profiling artists and activists who are making a difference in the cultural life of the community."

Tracing the arts boom, one could begin in Laguna Beach, with the expansion of the Laguna Moulton Playhouse and the rebuilding of the Laguna Art Museum (LAM); or with LAM's increased visibility and opportunity to attract a totally new audience at a smaller auxiliary museum set up at South Coast Plaza retail center, in rent-free space provided by C.J. Segerstrom & Sons.

Major expansions are also underway at Santa Ana's Bowers Museum and at Newport Beach's Newport Harbor Art Museum (NHAM). Shaking hands in 1987 with the Irvine Company, Orange County's largest landholder, NHAM's officials accepted a gift of 10 prime acres at the corner of MacArthur Boulevard and Pacific Coast Highway, south of the Irvine Company's Newport Center. The land for Newport Harbor Art Museum's first structure, built in 1977, was also contributed by the company.

Garden Grove's old gem of a movie house is another example of Orange County's fostering of the arts while at the same time preserving a bit of history. The Gem Theatre on Main Street and the accompanying arts complex include the restored Mills House gallery and an outdoor amphitheater, annually the summer scene of the Grove Shakespeare Festival, the only regularly performed Shakespeare (besides San Diego's Old Globe Theatre) in Southern California.

Directing worldwide attention to Laguna Beach, the city's annual Festival of the Arts (founded in 1939) includes the visually spectacular Pageant of the Masters, a series of "live" canvases and sculptures posed by unblinking dozens of Pageant veterans and newcomers. Dating from 1936, the Pageant commands international respect on a par with West Germany's "Passion Play," which is performed every 10 years in the village of Oberammergau.

A new twist on an old idea took place in Laguna Beach when the Trey Ligon Gallery opened in 1987 (LAT 3/16/87), mixing hallowed traditional artists like Rembrandt and Renoir with period furniture and other antiques. "I'm trying to set the trend," said 23-year-old Trey Ligon. "In ten years every art dealer will sell furniture."

Setting trends seems to prevail in Orange County. Although the number of dinner theaters nationwide dropped about 30 percent between 1984 and 1987—prompting *Orange County Businessweek* (1/19/87) to report that "the public seems to be losing its appetite for swallowing culture with cuisine"—Orange Countians support four dinner theaters: Harlequin Dinner Playhouse in Santa Ana, Grand Dinner Theatre in Anaheim, The Southampton in San Clemente, and Elizabeth Howard's Curtain Call Dinner Theater in Tustin.

In addition, Baxter's Street Restaurant in Newport Beach and Tibbie's Music Hall in Huntington Beach offer staged entertainment with food fare.

Continuing indications of the county's blooming, booming arts are apparent in activities like the appointment of a board of directors to Buena Park's cultural arts foundation; a proposal to San Clemente's city council to build a city cultural complex; and the City of Irvine's construction of a 750-seat theater located near the University of California on a site offered by UCI in 1983.

Even the world of high technology has caught the acting bug. Odetics Repertory Theatre, made up of a group of employees at Odetics, Inc., an Anaheim firm specializing in advanced electronics, presents an annual play, which, participants concede, is "amateur in standing but professional in our hearts" (LAT 3/20/87).

What started out in 1980 as "more or less of a morale booster [designed to] bring a sense of fun to the workplace and promote camaraderie," evolved into an in-house hit, as Odetics' employee-actors sought to experience the challenge of repertory theater while at the same time becoming more involved socially.

Orange Countians' love for the arts, however, is closely rivaled by their demand for education. Much time and energy are expended as students young and old fill the county's classrooms. Three-fourths of the population have some college, motivated by the eleven colleges and universities blanketing the county, offering undergraduate, postgraduate, and doctoral programs in the arts, business, medicine, and science.

Four well-organized and expanding community college systems (two-year schools operating as part of the public school system) conduct year-round adult classes during day and evening hours that offer instruction in a variety of subjects.

A potpourri of independent academic institutions, self-help learning centers, vocational training and regional occupational programs, and a public school system second to none nationally, complete Orange County's commitment to education.

The University of California at Irvine, Chapman College in Orange, and California State University in Fullerton are the major groves of academe. Each are engaged in growth that entails a need for physical expansion. And, in view of the county's increasing population and the interrelationship between education and the business community, each school promotes an agenda calling for coordination between higher education's curriculum and the county's employment needs.

In addition to science, engineering, business and management, and strong liberal arts listings, athletics also play an important part in all Orange County school programs. *MetroGuide* writer Jim Dean notes that numerous Olympic stars (including Bobby Webster, two-time gold medalist in platform diving, and world-class diver Greg Louganis) have emerged from the county's sports departments. One of the most celebrated stars is John Huarte, a former Heisman Trophy winner who played quarterback in the 1960s for Notre Dame's football team.

Commenting that "Orange County's community college athletic program is rated among the best of its kind in the nation," Dean adds:

Football, basketball, track and field, baseball, water sports, and soccer are major school programs, and teams and individuals compete for California Interscholastic Championships . . . Gifted athletes have opportunities to attract scholarship assistance from major colleges. Several Orange County community college football teams have competed in the Junior Rose Bowl classic.

Athletics is not confined, however, to school environments. Acknowledging that he has "always been a jock," Anaheim sporting goods distributor Larry Alpert believes that physical fitness, in addition to being good for the individual, directly affects Orange County's economic health. Exclaims Alpert:

No question! It's very important to keep the body in shape to do the rest of this, and I think that Orange County is sensational in being able to do that. We have miles and miles of bike trails, and miles of ocean. It's convenient to get to the foothills; there's golf, tennis—there's not a sport that's not available to us.

Taking fitness a step further and demonstrating Orange Countians' spirit and involvement in the community—part of the intrinsic *something* mentioned earlier that sets Orange County apart—older citizens, too, find ways of contributing and, they say, "exercising our minds" (LAT 2/6/87).

Gene Kadow, for example, is not ready for retirement and has a "thriving real estate business in Huntington Beach." Bob Gaskins, executive vice president of Eiki International in Laguna Niguel, has given "some thought" to retiring, but says he "prefers the business world." Les Giauque (pronounced "juke") drives 80 miles three days a week from San Diego County to his job in Fountain Valley, where he is the managing trustee at PM Management Services Company (a subsidiary of Pacific Mutual Life Insurance).

SCORE (Service Corps of Retired Executives, a department of the U.S. Small Business Administration) maintains an office in Santa Ana and is staffed with dozens of qualified not-so-retired people who lend their expertise and counsel in a wide range of business categories.

On a lighter note, Janet L. Schwartz, mother of five and grandmother of five, "paints her face white with a red heart on her cheek" and performs as a mime at schools and before senior citizens (LAT 3/22/87). "Besides entertaining them, the one point I try to get across to seniors is to keep busy," she says.

Ladling up love and hope with homemade chicken soup is Mary McAnena's way of reaching out (OCR 3/24/87). In her mid-eighties, the Irish "grandmother" of Hart Park in Orange uses money from her savings and pension to buy food, which she then prepares daily and serves to the homeless people who gather at the park's picnic tables.

Bran muffins fueling their get-up-and-go, a dozen men—eight over 70 years old and four over 80—participated in the 1987 Orange County-to-Las Vegas Senior Fitness Run, a 286-mile trek organized by Bill Selvin. Now in his late seventies, former track coach Selvin teaches fitness to Orange County senior citizens. Of their annual long-distance runs, Selvin told the *Los Angeles Times* (2/1/87), "We sleep, we eat, we horse around."

Agreeing that they are "just a bunch of characters," but adding a bit of esoteric insight, Bert Williams, a former Chapman College professor and the runners' resident philosopher, observes: "There isn't too much opportunity for adventure anymore. Getting out at 2 or 3 in the morning under the stars and [the] still, night desert air gives you a chance for meditation."

* * *

People in Orange County have innumerable opportunities for physical, social, and cultural development, as well as for intellectual growth. Many spend hours—quietly and almost unnoticed—in volunteer service or performing duties beyond what is expected of them. Only the surface has been scratched in this chapter to give the reader some idea of the fullness of Orange County's lifestyle.

Drawing a parallel between Orange County's growth and Chapman College's progress, President G.T. (Buck) Smith says:

The real meaning in life comes when you take what you have acquired and put it back into the system, or into the campus, or into the orchestra, or into the team, or whatever. And I think that's the very same maturation process that we're seeing in the county. There's a very high level of expectation from oneself . . . There's a qualitative dimension to life that requires—in fact, is an opportunity—for us to put back into the system.

Improving the quality of life is of genuine concern to Orange Countians, and they activate their interests by investing in ideas and people. In doing so Orange Countians have built not only a strong economic foundation but an environment for the *whole* person.

PAVING THE WAY TO THE FUTURE

IF CALIFORNIA IS THE ECON-
OMY OF THE FUTURE, THEN
ORANGE COUNTY IS CER-
TAINLY ONE OF ITS MAJOR
COMPONENTS.

—MICHAEL A. HENOS,

3i VENTURES

Describing the exciting, innovative spirit that has transformed Orange County from an agricultural economy into a multi-dimensional industrial, technological, and service economy is not difficult. However, keeping up with those countywide changes is, because Orange County—a microcosm of California's economic influence—is rapidly developing as a model for the next century of American business.

The county's diverse economy has enabled it to develop one of the highest per capita incomes in the nation, and to maintain one of the lowest (about 4 percent) unemployment rates. The county's 786 square miles (75 percent is privately owned) also represents one of the nation's fastest growing business environments.

A *Los Angeles Times* special report (5/3/87) indicates that by some estimates "job growth in Orange County should continue to outstrip national rates by 2 to 1."

During the past decade, the article continues,

the county has led much of the nation in growth in the service sector, electronics, high-tech manufacturing and medical technology. It is these expanding industries that economists believe will anchor the nation's economy in the 21st century—replacing aging manufacturing businesses.

California Employment Development Department statistics confirm that statement. The county's manufacturing employment during the

FACING PAGE: Traffic creates a ribbon of light on the 405 Freeway at MacArthur, looking toward Irvine.
Photo by Chris Bryant

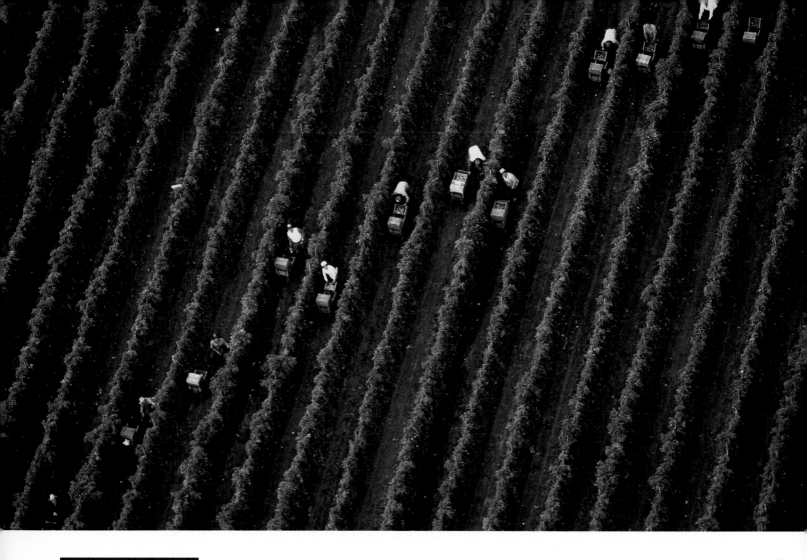

past 10 years has fallen to 23.1 percent from 26.1 percent. Likewise, government employees for the same period shrank to 10.6 percent of the work force from 14.8 percent.

In the industries considered crucial to a healthy economic future—technology, services, and international trade—Orange County already experiences a significant edge as combined employment for 1986 reached 56 percent of the work force, compared to 48 percent nationwide. "These are the industries in which we can compete worldwide," said James Doti, dean of Chapman College's school of business and management (LAT 5/3/87). "The unique composition of Orange County's economy is the shape of things to come."

Economic growth, especially in the high technology and medical industries, coupled with the county's evolving world trade position, fuels demands for specialized support in complementary and essential professions like banking, venture capital, accounting, and legal services, among others (see Chapter 4). In turn, new and expanding businesses multiply the demand for housing, entertainment, education, and retail and food services.

"The county has come full circle in the last thirty years and it takes a variety of talents, people, and networks to make that happen," says Michael A. Henos, a venture capitalist with 3i Ventures (Investors in Industry, Newport Beach). "The single most impressive thing about Orange County is a conscious effort by people to create an infrastructure for conducting and developing business efficiently."

Maintaining that smaller companies are "the engines that really facilitate economic growth and probably create more jobs annually than larger companies," Henos claims that "an entrepreneur can go from

A to Z without ever leaving the county, in terms of finding capital, marketing partners, manufacturers, services—the whole works. If California is the economy of the future, then Orange County is certainly one of its major components."

According to Wells Fargo Bank's 1986 forecast of the California economy, Orange County's average annual growth will outpace that of the state over the next 15 years. Let us look at some industries responsible for that growth, and review the economic cornerstones calculated to pave Orange County's way to the future.

HIGH TECHNOLOGY

Depending on whose survey you read, and whether it is ranking the nation's or California's high technology industry, Orange County comes in second or third, sometimes fourth. With approximately 2,000 technology companies currently to its credit, it does not really matter where on the high-tech tally you peg Orange County, for it is quite obviously top-notch.

The aerospace industry alone (defined by the California Employment Development Department as office, computing, and accounting machines; communications and electronics manufacturing; aircraft, missiles, and space vehicles; and measuring/controlling instruments) represented over 37 percent of all manufacturing employment in 1985.

With $5 billion in annual sales, aerospace accounts for about 10 percent of the county's employment (roughly 96,000 jobs in 1987), and nearly 10 percent of the gross county product.

Ford Aerospace, Northrop Corporation, Rockwell International, McDonnell Douglas Astronautics, and Hughes Aircraft, for example, are some of Orange County's largest single employers. These companies are not, however, simply aircraft assembly plants employing skilled and semi-skilled labor, but are manufacturers engaged in defense-related projects, which make up 35 percent of the nation's total space budget—a percentage which will most likely be allowed to grow rather than be cut, notes Earl S. Washington, vice president of Rockwell International, Anaheim (PSA 11/86).

Although the federal government's 1986 cuts in defense spending sliced through Orange County's aerospace contractors, effectively severing the industry's growth of past years and carving away at employment, major local firms continued to win defense contracts. This activity contributed to renewing Orange County's sagging electronics industry, but high-tech market analysts were loathe to predict a return to the high-flying days of the early 1980s, suggesting that the market may not realize sustained strong growth until 1988.

In the long run, however, defense-related businesses will contribute significantly to raising the county's total economic output to $86 billion by the year 2000, up 85 percent from $46.4 billion in 1985. That would mean an annual growth rate of 4.2 percent for Orange County, compared to California's projected rise of only 3.6 percent annually ($820 billion) for the year 2000.

The county's non-aerospace technology segment is smaller in size than the aerospace/defense segment, but it forms an equally important employment base. These firms manufacture products like lasers, robotics, fiber optics, computers, ceramics, and communications equipment. Hundreds of these companies nestle in the county's seventy-plus major industrial/commercial parks, companies like Odetics, Inc. in Anaheim (to date the manufacturer of the world's most advanced tape recorder used in space flight), American Businessphones, and AST Research (both located in Irvine and both ranked in the upper half of *Inc.* magazine's 1987 listing of the nation's 100 fastest-growing small public companies).

Orange County's cluster of non-aerospace technology companies (numbering 700, by some estimates) is considered by many to be a larger and more diverse concentration than that of Northern California's celebrated Silicon Valley.

For added prestige, Orange County's collection of companies in the medical technology industry is also without peer, statewide and nationally. In *PSA Magazine* (11/86), Dr. John E. Campion, vice president of Baxter Travenol Laboratories in Irvine, claims: "There are more than 450 individual biotechnology firms registered with the U.S. government within a ten-mile radius of the heart of Orange County, making this the largest concentration in the United States."

Stating that the county is an "incubator for the international biomedical industry," Campion says that "the county provides from 75 percent to 90 percent of such new equipment as heart valves, oxygenators, heart-lung bypass instrumentation, cardiovascular catheters, and equipment for search and laser surgery."

Orange County's international biomedical industry has developed over a 20-year period, Campion continues, with increasing activity during the last 10 years due largely to: farsighted local government, available land and buildings for development, strong academic institutions, one of the most highly educated and skilled work forces in the nation, an in-place high-technology infrastructure, and Orange County's "crown jewel"—risk takers and risk capital.

Adding to the litany of positives contributing to the last decade's growth in the technology industries, Robert P. Kelley, Jr., president and chief executive officer of SoCalTEN (Southern California Technology Executives Network, headquartered in Newport Beach), says:

High technology adds an incredible component of value per employee to the industries which it serves, and to that degree high tech will continue to draw highly skilled, professional employees to the area. Southern California, and Orange County in particular, will become dramatically attractive to high technology companies over the next ten years.

Why? Because, says Kelley, aside from the fact that Southern California is considered one of the most desirable places to live, "the number-one reason that Orange County will continue to attract high tech companies is its openness and integrity, which are essential characteristics for technology companies to grow."

Adaptability is the key, Kelley maintains. "Companies have to be able to address ever narrower product windows. We've developed a society here that's totally oriented towards change, and the characteristics of a society that enable it to constantly change and renew itself are honesty, integrity, and effective communication."

Although intense competition exists in each company's own market niche, Kelley says that a growing number of technology executives, in an exchange called peer mentoring, are "willing to share problems and opportunities in greater depth than formerly, concerning the develop-

A Hughes engineer inspects features of a billboard-sized air defense radar antenna. Courtesy, Hughes Ground Systems Group

ment of their companies and careers."

Calling Orange County "more collaborative in its business setting, compared to New York and Chicago, for example, or even Los Angeles," Kelley adds:

An open business culture that offers an opportunity to discuss critical issues concerning the development and survival of companies is going to be much more productive than a closed business environment, especially in creative endeavors like technology. And with greater emphasis being placed on Pacific Rim trade, companies realize that international competitors are far more of a potential problem to them than they are to themselves.

The concept of technology collaboration is being fostered by some local companies and by the American Electronics Association (AEA, a national trade organization representing a wide range of high technology firms). According to *Orange County Businessweek* (1/26/87), the AEA has formed a national aerospace and defense division to encourage such collaboration. Smaller companies can get a head start on their competition and make better use of their human resources by working with large manufacturers, says Don Osgood, the director of the Orange County AEA chapter's aerospace and defense division.

As technology advances and as more money is spent on research and development, with a longer delay for a profitable return, "we're reaching a point where, individually, we can't afford to take a lot of the risks," explains John R. Moore, vice president and general manager of Northrop's Electro Mechanical Division in Anaheim (OCB 1/26/87). He suggests that companies form joint ventures and consortiums similar to their Japanese and European competitors.

Joel Kotkin, the Los Angeles-based West Coast editor for *Inc.* magazine said Moore's suggestion highlights "Orange County's two psyches":

One is the old-fashioned psyche out of the 1950s; the traditionally conservative, white shoes, Sunbelt, hard-driving, entrepreneurial types. More recently, what you see is a technologically oriented, ethnically diverse type of business culture; people who are much more worldly than the traditional Orange County leadership.

Contrasting the county with "the other hottest high-tech area in the U.S., which is Silicon Valley," Kotkin explains that Orange Countians seem "a little more centered and come out of a somewhat more stable environment. Many worked in the aerospace industry or came from a large corporate background before starting their own companies."

The scintillating excitement surrounding Silicon Valley is absent in Orange County, "but that's a big advantage," Kotkin observes.

Whereas Silicon's culture has tended to be more fast growth, shoot from the hip, money made quickly, money lost quickly, high leverage, and much in the glare of publicity, Orange County businesspeople appear to be oriented towards the long term—more satisfied with building a $50 million company than blowing the wad on a $500 million company . . . I think you are better positioned for an economy that's going to become more internationally focused.

INTERNATIONAL FOCUS

Few would disagree that Orange County is becoming a pivotal force for international trade activity. An estimated one-third of the local companies providing products, services, and technologies are engaged in world trade at some level. Add to that a steady flow of foreign firms that are investing in commercial properties and establishing headquarters and regional distribution centers.

Take inventory of the growing acquisitions and mergers. Multiply by thousands the number of worldwide business contacts available through "Network," a computerized trade system offered by the World Trade Center Association of Orange County.

Calculate the benefits of the foreign trade zone in Santa Ana: new business, more jobs, revenue. (Approved in 1987 by the U.S. Department of Commerce, the 92-acre site east of the Civic Center is technically an extension of the Long Beach Trade Zone, which allows businesses and manufacturers in the zone to import duty-free raw materials. Duty is paid on the finished product only if it is sold in the U.S. If the item is sold abroad, no duty is assessed.)

Summing up, add in Orange County's proximity to commercial seaport terminals (at Los Angeles, Long Beach, and San Diego), access to domestic and international air services, the availability of major rail and surface transportation, and the county's location in the U.S. time zone closest to the Far East. The total: tremendous opportunity for "going global."

Although still a novice in developing world commerce, the county can already claim that 25 percent of its jobs are directly related to international business (compared to 10 percent statewide). "Companies that don't have an international agenda in their business plans won't be around twenty years from now," says Susan Lentz, executive director of the World Trade Center Association of Orange County.

"There are over 80,000 companies here and only 17 percent of them are interested in international business. This allows tremendous potential for foreign investment in the county, and for the growth and marketing of goods and services abroad."

Recognizing these facts, Coastline Community College applied for and received a U.S. Department of Education Title VI-B grant to study the training needs of international businesses operating in Orange County. As a result, and in a cooperative venture with the World Trade Center Association, Coastline Community College created a World Trade Center Institute to:

• further the research on international business potential in the county;

• act as a network, referral service, and clearinghouse for training and educational information on world trade;

• refer businesspeople to the appropriate and convenient training establishments;

• identify the training needs of Orange County's international businesses and develop programs in cooperation with educational institutions.

The enthusiasm with which the World Trade Center Institute has been received extends worldwide. Says Lentz, "Other world trade centers want to use it as a model."

The importance of improving the international educational aspects has not been lost on Orange County's other schools. Among them, the Irvine Unified School District (IUSD) educates what curriculum coordinator Bobbi Mahler calls "an interesting microcosm of the world, with thirty languages other than English spoken [among students]" (EX 4/86). All programs at IUSD, Mahler adds, "are influenced by the county's multi-national atmosphere."

The City of Orange's Chapman College has had a world focus since sending its first missionary graduates abroad in the late-nineteenth century. From 1965 to 1975 it sharpened its global awareness through its World Campus Afloat Program. The program, conducted aboard ship, sailed around the world twice a year. Today Chapman College is affiliated with exchange programs in England, Greece, and Spain, and has joined the International Student Exchange Plan, thus adding 65 universities in 35 nations to its exchange options.

"Chapman College is becoming more aggressive in providing study abroad programs for its students," says public relations director Jerry Derloshon, "and we are laying the groundwork for a junior-class study program abroad that will be required for all graduating Chapman College juniors."

The University of California, Irvine (UCI), California State University, Fullerton (CSUF), and the National Education Corporation (NEC) have also intensified their efforts to present business and management programs on a broader scale, including internships with foreign companies.

Orange County has made "the necessary transition from a rural backwater to a viable force in the international marketplace," said Martin Brower, editor and publisher of the *Orange County Report.* "By establishing a strong agricultural and business base with world ties, the county has managed the difficult leap from bean fields to global trade within the space of two short decades."

With foreign countries (especially Canada, Great Britain, France, Germany, Australia, Japan, and other Pacific Rim countries) seeking real estate, banking, retail, and other commercial investments in the county, Orange Countians are not leaving the finer points of international development to chance. Some companies, in fact, eager in the late eighties to take advantage of Japan's growing business presence, launched Pacific Rim marketing campaigns, hired consultants to tutor them on Japanese business customs, and produced video presentations and brochures in the Japanese language.

The county Board of Supervisors established the Orange County Office of Protocol in 1984, specifically to serve as a liaison with foreign consulates and to expand the area's world trade and investment opportunities, a goal that is enhanced by an annual economic conference designed to bring together the county's business community and the international consular corps. The event is co-sponsored with various local associations, including the World Affairs Council of Orange County, the Industrial League of Orange County, the World Trade Center Association, and the Orange County Chamber of Commerce.

Other organizations serving the multi-ethnic business community are the Hispanic Chamber of Commerce; the Asian American Business Association; a branch of the Japan Business Association of Southern California; and the Vietnamese Chamber of Commerce, whose objective, says the chamber's executive director, Loc T. Nguyen, is to provide assistance to the Indochinese who are relocating to the area, and to analyze business opportunities and explore the practical question of how to accelerate the flow of entrepreneurial talent in the Vietnamese community.

The most recent addition to Orange County's population, the Vietnamese community is estimated to be between 75,000 and 90,000 people. The commercial district—known as Little Saigon, which contains over 550 businesses—is located in a contiguous section of Westminster and Garden Grove. Reportedly the largest Vietnamese shopping district in the United States, Little Saigon serves not only Orange County but also Asians living throughout Southern California.

So much economic activity takes place in Orange County that reliable statistics are quickly outdated concerning the number of foreign companies arriving, or the number of firms going abroad. One indication, however, is membership in the World Trade Center Association, which opened its doors in 1976 with only 30 members, and in 1987 claimed 625.

But trends in trade change as swiftly as the wind, the late Thomas M. Self (a business writer and one of the founders in 1976 of *The Executive* magazine) once said, and "to determine how many foreign companies are headquartered in Orange County you need a daily newspaper and a scorecard."

FACING PAGE: Dramatic fountains accent the Koll Center grounds. Photo by Michele Burgess

Palms punctuate the grounds at Irvine Spectrum Mazda Headquarters. Photo by Jim Mendenhall

Historically, said Self (EX 4/86), Orange County's world trade was led 20 years ago by companies whose products and services were vital to the development of oil resources: Fluor Corporation, the Irvine-based engineering and construction firm; Smith International of Newport Beach; and Baker International Corporation and Varco International, both of Orange.

Following the oil-related firms, Self continued, technology and medical companies "moved with the speed of summer lightning in staking out international markets": China, Europe, the Middle East, Africa, the Far East, and Australia, among others. Beckman Instruments (now a subsidiary of SmithKline Beckman Corporation), Western Digital, Microdata Corporation (part of McDonnell Douglas Information Systems Group), Odetics, Inc., Irvine-based VLI Corporation, Dioptics Medical Products, and AST Research represent less than a thimbleful of Orange County's business globe-trotters.

As the county's overseas trade increased in the seventies, a similar movement was also taking place here, as Japanese companies began to establish factories, sales offices, and headquarters on the West Coast.

JAPANESE INVESTMENT

With increasing emphasis on Pacific Rim markets, Orange County's international fabric grows richer as Japanese companies increase their commercial investment in the region.

In the 1970s Japanese business was essentially attracted to cities lying closer to the Long Beach and Los Angeles harbors, and within easier reach of L.A.'s Japanese banks. Today an estimated 200 Japanese firms (of approximately 900 in Southern California) are located in Orange County, with Japanese banks at the forefront. Six (of 13 full-service Japanese banks in California) have established branches in the county: Mitsubishi, California First, Golden State Sanwa, Sumitomo, Mitsui, and Tokai. One Los Angeles banking consultant predicted that by 1990 every major Japanese bank would have regional offices in Orange County.

Dai Ichi Kangyo Bank of California (a U.S. subsidiary of the world's largest bank) has no branch in Orange County, yet has, since 1985, been active in financial matters. Most notably, it guaranteed a $69.5 million bond to provide streets, flood control, and other improvements for Westpark, a new residential community in the city of Irvine; and it issued a bond to finance roads, sewers, and other infrastructure for Irvine Spectrum, the 2,200-acre industrial/research/commercial complex under development by the Irvine Company (LAT 4/19/87). "A growing number of Japanese firms realize that [Orange County] is a strategically important place," said Hisao Kobayashi, chairman and president of Dai Ichi Kangyo Bank of California.

The California government does not keep statistics on a county-by-county basis, so a total figure for Japanese investment in Orange County is not available. The state's Department of Commerce reports, however (LAT 4/19/87), "that the value of property, plants and equipment owned by Japanese companies in California more than tripled from $1.2 billion in 1980 to $3.8 billion in 1984, the last year such information was tallied. About 60 percent of that investment has been made in the greater Los Angeles area, which includes Orange County."

Some of the reasons cited for selecting the county or relocating from the L.A. area include: safety; limited economic opportunities in Japan; lower land prices; clean, attractive office and industrial parks; a reputation as an important center for high technology manufacturing; and sophisticated research and development in fields like computers, electronics, medical instruments, and pharmaceuticals.

Exploring the county's crescive Japanese business community, the *Los Angeles Times* (4/19/87) reported that Kawasaki Motors Corporation/USA was one of the earliest Japanese companies to arrive, establishing offices in Irvine in March 1966. Others followed: Ricoh Electronics, Santa Ana, 1973; Mitsubishi Electric Sales America, Cypress, 1974; Calsonic, Irvine, 1976; Hitachi Consumer Products of America, Anaheim, 1979; Mitsubishi Electronics America, Santa Ana, 1980; Mitsubishi Motor Sales of America, Fountain Valley, 1981; Toshiba Industrial Electronics Business Sector, Irvine, 1981; and Mazda (North America), Irvine, 1981.

Recent Orange County acquisitions by Japanese firms, the *Times* said, include a number of significant purchases by Shuwa Investments Corporation (a major foreign contender in the county's real estate market since 1979): the 12-story Taco Bell headquarters building in Koll Center Irvine (1987; when the Taco Bell Corporation moved into the building in 1986, it was the largest office lease signed in Orange County history); a high-rise office building on MacArthur Boulevard, Irvine (1986); and the Downey Savings & Loan Association building in Costa Mesa (1986).

Also in Irvine, Chuo Mitsui Associates acquired a 50-percent owner-

Kazuo Ishiguro is the proud president of Toshiba. Photo by Yana Bridle

ship in the Burlington Air Express building in 1986; Toshiba America Industrial Electronics Business Sector purchased 26 acres in 1985 in Irvine Spectrum for construction of its national headquarters; and Canon USA bought 22 acres in Irvine Spectrum to accommodate its western regional headquarters.

Several miles west of the Irvine properties, in Santa Ana, Tobishima Development Company purchased nearly half of the 46-acre Hutton Centre. Located at Main Street and MacArthur Boulevard, the Tobishima acquisition included an eight-story office building and two restaurants.

As a sign of business stability, it is customary for Japanese firms to own (rather than rent) their properties, a practice that complements their host area's business attitude of committed, long-term investment. Many have enjoyed rapid growth in Orange County, requiring that they move to larger facilities. As they expand their commercial interests, it will mean more jobs for Orange Countians, because typically less than 10 percent of those employed by Japanese companies in the county are Japanese.

Already significantly involved in banking and manufacturing concerns, the Japanese are diversifying into hotels, life insurance companies, real estate development, and tourist-related enterprises. That kind of involvement, said one commercial broker, constitutes "more than a fly-by-night operation or 'Mickey Mouse' investment."

TOURISM
Disneyland's Magic Kingdom—and, yes, Mickey Mouse—put Orange County on the world's map in 1955, the same year that the Santa Ana Freeway opened.

Validating founder Walt Disney's opening-day statement that "Disneyland will never be complete as long as there's imagination left in the world," fun and fantasy from "the happiest place on earth" have since expanded from Anaheim's Disneyland to include Walt Disney World near Orlando, Florida (1971); the Experimental Prototype Community of Tomorrow (EPCOT, opened in Orlando in 1982); Tokyo Disneyland (1983); and Euro Disneyland (scheduled to open in 1992 on 4,800 acres located in Marne-la-Vallee, 18 miles east of Paris, France).

But Orange County's tourism economy comprises more than popular theme parks like Disneyland, or Knott's Berry Farm in Buena Park. It is a significant employer in the county.

Tourism (defined by the state's Employment Development Department as restaurants, hotels, and recreational facilities) increased its share of total wage and salary employment from 9.4 percent in 1979 to 10.7 percent in 1985, thus advancing from 76,600 jobs in 1979 to a 1985 total of 106,900 jobs. Figures released by the Anaheim Area Visitor & Convention Bureau for year-end 1986 indicate that 117,000 jobs (everything from restaurant help to airline presidents) were filled, and that figure is increasing at a pace of 4,000 more jobs per year.

The impact of tourism on Orange County is evident when one looks at the number of annual visitors: 34.6 million people "dropped by" in 1986 (a 5.5 percent increase over 1985) and spent nearly $5 billion (up 9 percent from 1985), which amounts to 10 percent of Orange County's overall economy. (Fifty-seven percent of the county's visitors hail from the western United States; 19 percent come from overseas.) Said

Founded by Walt Disney in 1955, Disneyland serves as host to thousands of visitors every year. © The Walt Disney Company

William Snyder (president of the Anaheim Area Visitor & Convention Bureau, which celebrated its twenty-fifth anniversary in 1987), "There is stiff competition for the visitor dollar, but we are confident that with a united effort we will build on our past successes and create a strong and bright future for the tourism industry in Anaheim/Orange County."

With 685,000 square feet of space (and plans for expansion to nearly one million square feet by the mid-1990s), the Anaheim Convention Center is the West Coast's largest exhibition hall. Surrounding hotels add another 360,000 square feet of available meeting space. (Orange County's second hub of hotels and motels, with additional accommodations for meetings and conferences, is in the Central-South County environs of Santa Ana, Costa Mesa, Irvine, and Newport Beach.)

Considered a superior location for some of the nation's foremost trade shows and conferences, the Anaheim Convention Center catered 294 conventions in 1986, totaling 925,350 delegates. It was, Snyder said, "the highest attendance figure in our history."

In terms of forthcoming bookings, the Convention Center reported early in 1987 that 283 conventions and trade shows had already reserved meeting space well into the next century.

While apparently "in the black," Orange County's tourist industry does not take itself for granted. Competing areas like Los Angeles, Long Beach, and San Diego constantly prod tourism officials into more prominent promotional campaigns and marketing strategies.

Recognizing that they have not always taken advantage of the potential tourist market, some attractions create joint promotions (like Disneyland and Knott's Berry Farm, which both opened new shows and

Dolphins leap on cue at the Pacific Pavilion at Knott's Berry Farm in Buena Park. Courtesy, Knott's Berry Farm

pleasure pavilions in 1986) and sharpen their marketing focus by pouring millions of dollars into television and print advertising and other forms of publicity. Often these marketing programs utilize the faces and names of highly visible sports and entertainment figures to sell Orange County's tourist industry to a worldwide audience. "We really have entered a whole new dimension [of marketing]," said Ron Kollen, Disneyland's advertising manager (OCR 4/19/87).

Another new dimension: hotels and the hospitality industry. As with the county's other rapidly developing economic segments, the push to construct more hotels, and to expand or refurbish old ones, stretches the imagination. Seventeen new hotels opened in 1986. Six more greeted 1987, adding 2,000 *chambres* to the existing 37,895 rooms.

Not surprisingly, as more hotel rooms became available than could immediately be absorbed, Orange County's occupancy rates for 1986 (and estimated through mid-1987) ran from 50 percent to 73.5 percent, with the established inns quoting the higher percentages.

Overall, however, both the hospitality industry and market analysts are optimistic about demand catching up with supply, as each new lodging settles into its market niche, and as future hotel construction eases. "We'll see the market begin to stabilize," said Boyd Lypka, senior consultant with Costa Mesa-based Laventhol & Horwath. Quoting an average occupancy rate of about 60 percent for year-end 1986, Lypka told the *Orange County Businessweek* (1/12/87) that for the number of hotels added, "that's pretty good. It shows a lot of the market's ability to absorb the new rooms."

With all the construction taking place throughout Orange County, the absorption of space—be it hotels, office buildings, industrial parks, or other development—always furrows someone's brow until the market

ABOVE: The Ritz Carlton Hotel provides a luxurious retreat in Laguna Niguel. Photo by Chris Bryant

LEFT: Relaxation and pleasant accommodations are offered at the Balboa Inn in Newport Beach. Photo by Michele Burgess

demand for the product begins to catch up. Talking about Orange County real estate development—like talking about the weather—is a daily occurrence.

REAL ESTATE

If interest rates were to drop by 3 percent, someone said in 1986, you would be able to walk from Los Angeles to San Diego on rooftops.

Real estate development is sometimes considered—only half in jest—as Orange County's primary economy. Without a strong real estate presence, many say, very little of the county's diversified economic offerings (which contribute to employment opportunities, to a stable labor force, and to attracting new business) would have been conceived, born, and brought to maturity.

For others, real estate development is the red flag signaling the unwanted arrival of more people, more business, and more traffic congestion. For many, that is an undesirable view, which has resulted in serious moves to restrain growth (see Chapter 6).

Lacking a conventional and well-defined urban area or "downtown," Orange County's 27 cities have evolved independently, producing among them several mini-metropolitan centers that reinforce each other and fit roughly into three geographic areas: the Greater Airport Area (primarily Newport Beach and Irvine); South Coast Metro (Costa

LEFT: Cranes help erect a new office tower at the Lincoln Town Center in Santa Ana. Photo by Wayne de Hertoghe

FACING PAGE: Visitors can enjoy the hospitality of the Holiday Inn. Photo by Yana Bridle

Mesa and parts of Santa Ana); and Central County (Anaheim, Orange, Santa Ana, and Garden Grove).

The Greater Airport Area. Surrounded by farmland in the 1950s, a lonely community airport searchlight and a four-story office building on the corner of MacArthur Boulevard and Campus Drive were the tallest structures for miles around, and visible from the Santa Ana Freeway when Donald M. Koll (a third-generation Californian raised in Los Angeles) decided in 1958 that he wanted to live in Newport Beach, "even if it meant pumping gas," he recalled (EX 4/87).

(The four-story building is still used and was constructed by Laguna

RIGHT: Koll Center offers a colorful welcome. Photo by Jeff Marks

FACING PAGE: A new addition at Koll Center in Irvine is seen here under construction. Photo by Yana Bridle

Niguel-based Birtcher, a family-owned company with Orange County roots dating from 1909. Today, Birtcher is the nation's tenth-largest developer and the eleventh-largest property manager—OCR 7/5/87).

In 1968, 10 years after starting the Koll Company (one of the West Coast's largest corporations with interests in development, construction, asset management, and acquisitions), Don Koll sought joint venture partnerships with financial houses for the purpose of building business parks.

Making an unprecedented request that the investor put up 100 percent of the development funds while he supplied the construction, Koll chuckled, "I got thrown out of some pretty good offices before I got Aetna [Life & Casualty] as a partner."

The dusty land parcels that Koll presented to Aetna's skeptical management in 1968 ran along the (then) two-lane MacArthur Boulevard, south of the Santa Ana Freeway and adjacent to the community airport. "There's nothing out there!" they exclaimed (EX 4/87). "Someday," Koll replied, "it will be the Wilshire Boulevard of Orange County."

Aetna Life & Casualty joined Koll in his entrepreneurial venture to develop what is now called the MacArthur Corridor, and today—hundreds of projects later—the Koll Company is credited with getting the Greater Airport Area off the ground.

As for the single-searchlight community airport, it grew into John

Wayne Airport/Orange County, with the distinction of being one of the nation's busiest airports in terms of takeoffs and landings.

Along with Central County, the Greater Airport Area has the lion's share of the commercial office market, according to Grubb & Ellis's 1987 real estate report. By the end of 1986 Orange County had approximately 27 million square feet of multi-tenant speculative office space in buildings (larger than 25,000 square feet) constructed since 1975.

This inventory represented about 80 percent of the total 1986 Orange County office market, Grubb & Ellis reported, of which 54 percent was located in the 3,350-acre Irvine Business Complex (IBC contains some of Southern California's most important devel-

oped and undeveloped land). The airport area's office inventory is expected to double by 1995, reaching about 32 million square feet, "a mass second only to downtown Los Angeles in all of Southern California," said Richard M. Ortwein, president of the Koll Company's Newport Beach Division (PSA 11/86).

In 1986 eleven "of the most harmonious blend of developers I'm aware of," Ortwein said, formed the Irvine Business Consortium to market the IBC, as well as to tout the attributes of their individual projects. Patterned after the South Coast Metro Alliance (officially established in 1984 by C.J. Segerstrom & Sons in Costa Mesa), the IBC consortium includes regional and national developers: Robert A. Alleborn Associates, Birtcher, Brinderson Ltd., Douglas Development Company, French & McKenna Company, Legacy Companies, Irvine Company, Koll Company, McLachlan Investment Company, Prudential Development Group, and Trammell Crow Company.

Scores of banks, law offices, investment and accounting firms, as well as other professional services, supplement the Irvine Business Complex's multitude of business parks that contain research and development, industrial facilities, retail space, and corporate offices.

Combined with physical assets other than the airport and freeway access (like nearby housing and recreational opportunities, the University of California, and Irvine Spectrum, for example), the Greater Air-

RIGHT: Distinguished by its landmark tower, Park Place in Irvine is recognized as a complete business environment. Courtesy, Trammell Crow Company

FACING PAGE: The Irvine Company's Jamboree Center is pictured against a bold blue sky. Photo by Yana Bridle

port Area is viewed as one of Orange County's economic polestars.

The largest single development in the Irvine Business Complex is the $1-billion Koll Center Irvine, the Koll Company's 95-acre mixed-use commercial center situated on Von Karman Avenue. During the mid-1980s seven office buildings, a hotel, and three restaurants made an appearance; 1986 saw the completion of an Embassy Suites, a Holiday Inn, an 11-story National Education Corporation building, and Taco Bell Corporation's 12-story headquarters (purchased from the Koll Company in 1987, for $64 million, by Shuwa Investment Corporation, a Japanese firm).

Large master-planned developments like Koll Center Irvine (or the Irvine Company's Newport Center/Fashion Island and C.J. Segerstrom & Son's South Coast Plaza/Town Center) strive to attract people for evening pleasures as well as to provide daytime employment and services. To that end, company officials say, when Koll Center Irvine is completed in 1992 it will include 4 million square feet of office space, four hotels, up to 20 restaurants, a multiscreen cinema, expanded retail facilities, and a health club.

As developers pursue plans individually or team with each other to bring drawing board sketches to life, older projects are expanded and new ones rise in the cities of Newport Beach and Irvine, such as (but not all-inclusive): The Atrium (French & McKenna Company), Dupont Centre (Legacy Companies in a joint venture with BCE Development Corporation), Century Centre (Robert A. Alleborn Associates), Fluor Cor-

poration's headquarters site (purchased in 1985 by Dallas-based Trammell Crow); and the Irvine Company's MacArthur Court, Executive Park, and Jamboree Center.

(Historically, the Irvine Company incorporates a significant Orange County entity, which includes the creation of the city of Irvine, the nation's largest and most successful planned community. The company has extensive holdings in commercial, industrial, and residential properties in Newport Beach, Irvine, Tustin, and Orange.

(The organization's wealth and influence originated with James Irvine, Sr., who consolidated the Irvine Ranch holdings—more than 120,000 acres in 1876. Once embracing one-quarter of the county's land, the Irvine Company today retains about 68,000 acres, approximately one-sixth of Orange County, and has entered a new era of development goals under the leadership of Donald L. Bren, who acquired a majority interest in 1983.)

Eventually, in the Irvine Business Complex, Hillman Properties will build on a 68-acre site acquired from Smith Tool (in the Von Karman Corridor, north of the San Diego Freeway), and Birtcher (on the south end of the freeway) will develop a 15-acre site formerly occupied by Parker Hannifin's Bertea Control Systems division, which at one time considered moving its facilities out of Orange County, but in 1985 purchased 60 acres in Irvine Spectrum to build a 330,000-square-foot research, manufacturing, and assembly plant.

Considered a bold concept in terms of size and entrepreneurial en-

Parker Hannifin makes its home in Irvine Spectrum. Photo by Jim Mendenhall

deavors, the 2,200-acre Irvine Spectrum is the Irvine Company's international center for research, technology, and business. The design includes Irvine Center, an urban core which will combine corporate headquarters with hotels, theaters, shops, and restaurants.

The realization of the complex marks the first time that a major Orange County real estate developer has attempted to create the research and development environment usually associated with university interests. Consequently, as Orange County glides into the twenty-first century, Irvine Spectrum is viewed by many as establishing a new and productive relationship between business, education, science, and technology.

Located about eight miles southeast of the John Wayne Airport (at the triangle of the San Diego, Santa Ana, and Laguna Canyon freeways), parts of the complex have been under development since the 1970s. The original concept for a combined technology, biosciences, and commercial core was redesigned and renamed Irvine Spectrum in 1984, following extensive construction in the industrial portion and reevaluation by the Irvine Company concerning support services and the needs of the businesses locating in the complex.

Between 1977 and 1986, 340-plus companies (with a capital investment of more than $500 million, and 13,000 employees) settled in Irvine Spectrum, thus forming a remarkably wide range of enterprise constituting a broad economic base.

Irvine Spectrum's magnets to attract firms include alliances with the University of California, Irvine; the construction of two specialized centers: the National Academies of Sciences and Engineering and the Irvine Medical Center, a teaching and community hospital built and operated by American Medical International (AMI); proximity to the Irvine Business Complex, one of the largest concentrations of high technology companies in the U.S.; and Orange County's strategic placement at the crossroads of Southern California's activity with Pacific Rim countries.

Irvine Spectrum offers space for start-up companies as well as for those that are expanding or relocating. From the fall of 1985, and extending over a 16-month period, a significant cadre of local businesses and a collection of national and international companies established themselves in Spectrum at the rate of at least one new company per week.

Reinforcing Irvine Spectrum's ability to draw tenants, John Shumway (vice president of Market Profiles, an independent real estate analysis company in Costa Mesa) said that "Spectrum may have 45 percent of the new industrial leases in the county" (OCB 6/22/87). The majority of new additions, Shumway added, came from the county, but a large number of Japanese and other Asian companies were also signing leases.

(The county has over 130 million square feet of industrial space according to the 1987 Grubb & Ellis real estate report, which defines industrial space as standard manufacturing and distribution facilities, high technology research and development buildings, plus a percentage of office space and parking.)

An important aspect of Irvine Spectrum, one that keeps its development moving ahead and on schedule according to company officials, is the venture partnerships between the Irvine Company and other major real estate developers. The company has joined with the Koll Company, Legacy Companies, Sammis Company, Birtcher, and O'Donnell, Brigham & Partners/Southern, for example, in the construction of restaurants, retail, high technology, and bioscience buildings.

In keeping with the Irvine Company's philosophy to respect a balance between industrial development and the human factor, Irvine Spectrum is supported by a system of open space, housing, transportation improvements, and employment.

Mention must be made of one of the Irvine Company's most impressive "developments" in the Greater Airport Area, an elaborate marketing tool named, prosaically, the Irvine Exhibit.

Designed for the Irvine Company by the David H. Gibson Company in Dallas, Texas, the multi-media, multi-million dollar Irvine Exhibit occupies 20,000 square feet on two floors at the company's Jamboree Center in Irvine, and depicts the corporation's residential, commercial, and industrial sites, including demographics and anticipated growth.

The Irvine Exhibit opened in June 1986, and a year later had welcomed over 7,000 visitors. The display offers a kaleidoscopic array of multi-image slide presentations, wall-mounted maps, floor-to-ceiling project models, and a 15-foot square resolution map/model of the Irvine Company's existing and planned structures in the communities of Irvine, Newport Beach and portions of Costa Mesa, Santa Ana, Tustin, El Toro, Lake Forest, Laguna Hills, and Laguna Beach. The model's detail is so precise that visitors can locate their homes or offices.

Moving away from the immediate airport surroundings, towards the Pacific Ocean and a bluff overlooking Newport Bay, one arrives at the Irvine Company's Newport Center. Hemmed between MacArthur Boulevard (east) and Jamboree Road (west) where they dovetail with the Pacific Coast Highway, the center (developed in the late sixties) contains 800 companies and 13,000 employees, and is described by Martin Brower as "the third point of south-central Orange County's prestige office and hotel triangle" (in relation to the Irvine Business Complex located east of the John Wayne Airport, and South Coast Metro situated west of the airport).

In *PSA Magazine* (11/86), Brower said the 450-acre mixed-use Newport Center

is certainly one of the most beautiful in the world, with a series of in-

dividually designed office towers, low-rise office and restaurant centers, medium towers and hotels—many of the buildings with superb views of spectacular Newport Bay—encircling, across a palm tree-lined divided roadway, Newport Center's Fashion Island shopping center.

"The Irvine Company is working hard," Brower added, "to continue the shopping center as a complex that serves the entire community, and to get away from its 'Rodeo Drive South' image" [referring to Los Angeles's exclusive shopping district].

But it is difficult to change the perception of Fashion Island's retail center, Brower continued, given the posh shops ensconced in the recently constructed Atrium Court, or Amen Wardy's high-fashion designer clothes salon, and the Rolls-Royce-type cars that appear in valet parking.

Running second to Costa Mesa's South Coast Plaza in terms of sales revenue, Fashion Island's million-dollar-plus mid-eighties renovation, which included additional retail space and new restaurants, boosted 1986 retail sales to approximately $225 million, up 13 percent from 1985.

Moving west from the Greater Airport Area to portions of Santa Ana and Costa Mesa, a 3.5-square-mile section designated as South Coast Metro has emerged as Orange County's second important economic center, with respect to the amount and quality of development and the type of tenants.

South Coast Metro. "This little 'city' is extremely visible," said Ted Fuller, the senior vice president-manager of Johnson & Higgins, a national insurance firm (EX 4/85). "Various metropolitan areas have one or two things that set them apart, but what's being built here and the total cultural enhancement in one location hasn't occurred anyplace else that I know of. It's extremely exciting, and I think developers and other people are making it even more so."

Comprising parts of the cities of Santa Ana and Costa Mesa, South Coast Metro's roots date from the early 1900s when lima beans and other agricultural products graced the land. Today, north of MacArthur Boulevard between Bristol Street and Harbor Boulevard, only a few hundred acres of limas survive. A bean warehouse belonging to developer C.J. Segerstrom & Sons—its dull gray concrete accented by turquoise loading chutes—stands at the intersection of Alton and Greenville, two-lane streets within hailing distance of the San Diego Freeway.

The Metro's 2,240 acres are easily accessible via four criss-crossing freeways or major intra-Orange County avenues, and John Wayne Airport is only a few minutes' drive from most Metro destinations.

If the success of any sizable property development were solely dependent—in real estate brokers' language—on location, location, location, then the Metro would certainly qualify as a success. But location alone is not enough to explain the Metro's dynamic growth. George Argyros, president of Arnel Development Company (and the developer of Metro Pointe) said in *The Executive* magazine (4/85):

There is a unique strength in the joint cooperation between the public and private sector. It's a continuing theme and I must compliment the City of Costa Mesa on its tremendous foresight to encourage the kind of development it's finally getting there. Not only did city government recognize opportunity, but they acted upon it, and that is very refreshing.

Credit for the original activity spawning the growth of South Coast Metro lies with C.J. Segerstrom & Sons, a family-owned partnership whose ancestors left Sweden in 1882 and settled briefly in the Midwest. In 1898 Charles John Segerstrom brought his family of 12 to Orange County.

During the family's first 50 years in agricultural operations in the county it maintained two of California's largest dairy farms (which were sold in 1942) and pioneered the commercial production of large lima beans.

In 1948, according to company history, the Segerstroms purchased from the United States Government (in a sealed bid auction) 76 acres of land along Harbor Boulevard in Costa Mesa, which included 110,000 square feet of warehouse buildings and a 2 1/2-mile spur of railroad line.

In 1953 (the same year that public hearings and planning began for the San Diego Freeway), 800 acres of land served by the Segerstrom-owned rail line were re-zoned by the Orange County Board of Supervisors for industrial development, marking the county's first major industrial land zoning (in northwest Costa Mesa: Harbor Boulevard to Fairview Road, and Warner Street to the San Diego Freeway).

Today, C.J. Segerstrom & Sons owns and manages property in Santa Ana, Tustin, and Costa Mesa, but the most prominent display of the developer's projects are in the South Coast Metro, where Town Center (site of the Orange County Performing Arts Center, the South Coast Repertory Theatre and other entertainment, and the heart of the area's professional and financial services corps) and South Coast Plaza/Crystal Court retail center form the backbone of the Metro's urban growth.

Declared an official tourist destination in 1987 by American Airlines for a summer tour package (a first in the airline industry), South Coast Plaza emporium runs to nearly 3 million square feet and is deemed one of the nation's most successful shopping centers, with projected 1987 annual sales of $735 million.

Aerial photos taken of South Coast Metro show that in 1980 only six major developments had risen between Bristol and Bear streets since 1960: South Coast Plaza (1967, one of Southern California's earliest enclosed regional retail centers); South Coast Plaza Village (1973, developed by C.J. Segerstrom & Sons north of the retail center, across Sunflower Avenue, in Santa Ana); South Coast Repertory Theatre (1978, privately funded, constructed on land contributed by the Segerstrom family); Downey Savings and Loan (1978); Westin South Coast Plaza Hotel (1975, owned jointly by C.J. Segerstrom & Sons and Connecticut General Life Insurance); and Imperial Bank (1979, joint venture between C.J. Segerstrom & Sons and the Prudential Insurance Company of America).

Richard N. Frost, a partner in the commercial brokerage company of Frost Trinen Partners, located in Town Center, said that the development of the Metro "sort of snuck up on most people—but not Henry" [H.T. Segerstrom, grandson of the founder and a managing partner in C.J. Segerstrom & Sons —EX 4/85]. Declaring that Henry Segerstrom was a "visionary" for perceiving the area's commercial potential, Frost added, "He was planning developments on a ten-year scale when other people were thinking about projects only two, three, or five years down the road."

ABOVE: The Irvine Company, which is the largest developing company in Orange County, developed Newport Center in its entirety. The Atrium Court is a recent addition. Photo by Michele Burgess

RIGHT: Shopping and dining are a pleasure in the airy Atrium at Newport Center. Photo by Yana Bridle

Recalling the rural ambience of the late 1970s that surrounded the opening of the Westin South Coast Plaza Hotel (originally referred to as "Henry's Folly"), and considered the catalyst for further development in the area, Frost said (EX 4/85), "You have to remember that Newport Beach and the airport corridor were the desirable addresses then. People questioned putting a hotel in a vacant bean field . . . The prevailing attitude was that only small commercial businesses would locate here."

The small commercial businesses did locate in South Coast Metro. But also, in the intervening years, more and larger construction projects began to replace the agricultural products: six new hotels (Red Lion, Beverly Heritage, Compri, La Quinta, the Marriott's Courtyard, and the

Residence Inn); restaurants and movie theaters; the Orange County Performing Arts Center (see Chapter 2); the Artists Center (a wing added to South Coast Repertory Theatre); the half-moon-shaped, 21-story Center Tower (with views of the Pacific Ocean, less than 10 miles away); and numerous other high-rise office structures housing tenants of every stripe—Big Eight accounting firms, national law offices and insurance companies, and financial institutions (representing over $3 billion in assets in 1985).

Adding significantly to the Metro's move from bean fields to board rooms, a half-dozen developers in September 1984 launched the South Coast Metro Alliance. It was Orange County's first such cooperative attempt by competing companies to promote a particular area, and the idea has since been emulated in the Irvine Business Complex and elsewhere.

Recent developments by the Alliance's growing membership include:

Casual dining and an abundance of shops are offered at South Coast Metro. Courtesy, South Coast Metro

Crystal Court, west of South Coast Plaza (C.J. Segerstrom & Sons); South Coast Executive Centre (QB Properties and Johnson Wax Development); South Coast Corporate Center and Lake Center (California Pacific Properties); Harbor Corporate Park (Sammis Company); Metro Pointe (Arnel Development); and South Coast Metro Center (Transpacific Development Company).

At the eastern boundary of South Coast Metro (where the Newport-Costa Mesa Freeway joins MacArthur Boulevard), at Hutton Centre, new projects will be completed before the end of the eighties by South Coast Metro Alliance members Griffin Realty Corporation, Hutton Development Company/Tobishima Development Company, and PacTel Properties.

South Coast Metro's development may not have been "worth

FACING PAGE: An office building
rises near the performing arts center. Photo by John Sanford

beans" during the 1960s and early 1970s, but it certainly flourished later and during the 1980s, illustrating the value of patience and planning. Said Henry Segerstrom during a rare interview in 1986, "The one thing you learn in farming is patience. You don't plant something and have it come to maturity in twenty-four hours. It takes time; especially in real estate development, time is one of the essential ingredients."

Central County. Although the Greater Airport Area and South Coast Metro have captured most of the headlines concerning commercial and office market development, Central County is a worthy contender, rising fast in recent years.

Encompassing portions of the cities of Anaheim, Orange, Santa Ana, and Garden Grove, "Central County is becoming a hub of office, retail, and even hotel development," wrote Martin Brower in *PSA Magazine* in November 1986. "While not attracting the prestigious service firms, [it] *is* attracting big-name insurance companies and 'backroom' operations of the Fortune 500."

Tishman West Management Corporation (manager of The City, a mixed-use commercial complex in Orange) was one of the first developers involved in the area, Brower said, "and for many years faced only small-developer competition . . . Now other developers are rushing into the market. Included are: The Koll Company, Birtcher, JMB/Federated with Henry Segerstrom, and Tishman Realty (not affiliated with Tishman West). Smaller developers, such as Nexus, are having a heyday."

Other development for Central County, documented in Brower's 1986 economic report for *PSA Magazine*, include: The City Tower, a 20-story office building; Birtcher's TriCenter, which is located in Anaheim near Anaheim Stadium, at the confluence of the Santa Ana and Orange freeways; and the Plaza Alicante complex in Garden Grove (which includes the Hyatt Regency Alicante hotel), developed by Beauchamp Development.

In Orange, The City (across from the University of California Medical Center) leased corporate headquarters space in 1986 to Bergen Brunswig, a large drug distributor (formerly located in Los Angeles's Century City).

Also in Orange, the Koll Company is developing a 21-acre site within the Southwest Redevelopment Plan. When completed in 1996, the $300 million Koll Center Orange will have 1.3 million square feet of office space in four office towers, a 260-room hotel, two restaurants, a two-level athletic club, and three parking structures.

Orange County's office and commercial real estate development is ongoing and all pervasive, as subcenters open up in the cities of Anaheim Hills, Yorba Linda, Brea, Cypress, and Huntington Beach, as well as in South County, where still-vacant rolling hills tease developers' imaginations to design interdependent urban villages, which combine a total living and working environment (see Chapter 6).

The preceding economic cornerstones—high technology, international trade, Japanese investment, tourism, and real estate—are destined to pave Orange County's future, but not alone. An essential complement of this economic development is the services industry.

Let us turn now to the bulwark of professional services that constitute another sort of economic cornerstone for Orange County's economy.

PROFESSIONAL PANACHE

WHAT SETS ORANGE COUNTY
APART IS ITS BUSINESS CORE;
A COMPLETE, FULL-SCOPE
BUSINESS COMMUNITY.

—RONALD L. MERRIMAN,

PEAT MARWICK MAIN & CO.

The Orange County business community's changing economic landscape includes a dynamic services industry that has taken on a life of its own in terms of excellence and far-sighted professional preparation.

Strongly reinforcing the area's economic and social structure in such fields as accounting, law, personnel, retail, advertising and public relations, medical and dental care, health care, finance, and venture capital, the services industry accounts for over three-fourths of all jobs in Orange County.

The largest job gains to date were recorded between 1984 and 1985, with increases in the services industry totaling 10,600, according to the California Employment Development Department's 1986-1987 annual planning information. Total employment in the services sector rose to an average of 232,300 jobs in 1985. The Chapman College Economic Business Review (December 1986) estimated that in 1987 the county's service industries would add 34,200 jobs.

Reflecting on the county's integrated growth through the years, Art Kidman, a senior partner at Rutan & Tucker (Orange County's oldest law firm) says, "This county has reached a real point of what everybody calls synergism; it's a place by itself now. It only lacks two things to really make it a completely separate identity from Los Angeles: a major airport and independent electronic media."

Since 1936, when Alexander W. Rutan and James B. Tucker linked legal expertise and formed Rutan & Tucker, the firm has developed a diverse clientele that matches the county's transition from agriculture to industry, real estate development, and construction. "The long-term strength of Rutan & Tucker," Kidman says, "has been in representing

FACING PAGE: Diners enjoy the Ritz's fine food and fine service. Photo by Yana Bridle

the landed gentry. Originally, as the county changed, so did the law firm. As the land was developed and a greater need for government infrastructure and provisions for community services arose, that opened an area of legal consultation that Rutan & Tucker put a lot of emphasis on."

During the late 1960s, when the county began developing as a financial center, "our law firm followed along in that respect as well," Kidman continues, "refining its capabilities to advise bankers and other people involved in financial situations where they need to raise money in securities offerings."

With 110 lawyers at Rutan & Tucker's Costa Mesa offices in the Central Bank building, near South Coast Plaza, the firm's public and private clients can seek a range of services in real estate, finance, public law, and related litigation that founder Rutan would hardly have dreamed of when he started practicing law in the county in 1906.

Like many Orange County enterprises, Rutan & Tucker made a commitment early in its history "to grow with the economy of the county," says Kidman, "and part of that pledge was a commitment to excellent professional services (because we didn't want to refer clients elsewhere for lack of expertise), which has been realized by recruiting the best talents and skills from major law schools around the U.S."

Competition for first-rate legal minds and clients is intense in Orange County, Kidman notes, as law firms expand their services and as seasoned lawyers leave established firms to start their own law practices, of which a dramatic example was the departure of 18 lawyers in April 1987 from the Newport Beach branch of Gibson, Dunn & Crutcher (a Los Angeles-based firm with no previous "departees" in its 97-year history) to form their own practice in Irvine (Pettis, Tester, Kruse & Krinsky). Saying that the time was right to make the break, economically, due to Orange County's growth, Alan W. Pettis told the *Los Angeles Times* (4/28/87), "If we start with a new venture now, we can be part of that growth."

Spin-off firms (including at least two from Rutan & Tucker, whose "alumni" include the 50-lawyer firm of Stradling, Yocca, Carlson & Rauth in Newport Beach, and the 40-lawyer firm of Drummy, Garrett in Costa Mesa) and the occasional transfer of outside law firms' top corporate lawyers to Orange County's branch offices, illustrate well the legal profession's maturing status. But even greater evidence of the increasing importance of the county's legal business is apparent in the number of "local outposts" being set up by major law firms from other cities, including Dallas, Houston, Cleveland, Minneapolis, and San Francisco.

Since 1980, the number of law firms has increased from 400 to 670; the number of lawyers has risen from about 4,500 to 7,500, and is expected to grow by 500-plus per year for at least several more years. The Orange County Bar Association, which 15 years ago met in a local Elks Lodge, today has 4,000 members who meet in their own 5,500-square-foot building that is currently undergoing renovation and expansion.

Like law firms, advertising and public relations companies are also making a name for themselves in Orange County, and are gradually debunking the notion that only Los Angeles or Chicago or New York can provide sophisticated marketing communications.

Since Orange County was built by and subsists on risk-taking indi-

viduals, it is only proper that the county's largest advertising agency—
Cochrane Chase, Livingston & Company—would also be established
and advanced by entrepreneurs catering to entrepreneurs. And, of
course, a tale is attached to the company's beginning.

In 1965 Cochrane Chase entered the advertising business as vice president of Newport Advertising in Newport Beach. He spent a year at the
agency before deciding to start his own company (LSC 4/84). "That's
wonderful," his wife reportedly said, on learning the news. "What kind
of clients do you have?" "I don't have any," Chase answered. So (the
story goes) they counted their money and decided they could survive
for six or eight months until the agency jelled.

The local legend is that Chase traded a pair of wing-tip shoes for his
first ad layout. Four lean months followed, said the *Liberty Street Chronicle*, then he took home a $100 paycheck. At the end of his first year
(1966) he was paying himself $600 a month, and had five clients and
$41,000 in billings.

In 1987, at the end of 21 years, Cochrane Chase, Livingston & Company claimed about $70 million in annual billings. It is one of the world's

top 100 largest ad agencies since being purchased in 1984 by London-
based Satchi & Satchi Compton Worldwide. Cracking the top 100 list
was President Lynn Livingston's dream (he joined the agency in 1971
as a copywriter and account executive—SCM 5/87). "We figured that
once we made the top 100, we'd really be doing something," he dead-
panned. "We just didn't know what that something was, but once we
figure it out, we'll really be dynamite."

A decade ago, toying with the idea of putting their headquarters elsewhere, Chase and Livingston asked themselves where the economic
growth would take place, and "after plotting things out, we felt it would
occur right here," Livingston said (SCM 5/87). With the influx of national and international companies since their decision, the partners are
"extremely pleased that business is moving into the Orange County area.

Stately Victorian homes line this
Huntington Beach avenue. Photo
by Yana Bridle

[It has] really become the hot spot for a lot of business—certainly the med/bio/science-type businesses [and] the high-tech-type businesses, [and] now some of the service-oriented businesses. We couldn't be happier."

Similar to the failure of some outside law firms to successfully break into the Orange County marketplace because of its inherent loyalty to local lawyers, Los Angeles advertising agencies also find it difficult to establish a foothold in the Orange County market. The reason, Livingston thinks (SCM 5/87), is because "sometimes L.A. has the tendency to think very much like New York. You can't do that in Orange County … [You have to take] the time to understand the entrepreneurial nature of the market."

Advice well taken, apparently, by several of Orange County's larger agencies (OCR 2/15/87), including (with annual billings; some are estimates): Reiser Williams deYong, Irvine, $40 million; Basso & Associates, Newport Beach, $24.5 million; Jansen Associates, Santa Ana, $22 million; Stiller Advertising, Costa Mesa, $14.5 million; Salvati Montgomery Sakoda, Santa Ana, $14 million; Lenac, Warford, Stone, Newport Beach, $14 million; B.J. Stewart Advertising, Newport Beach, $13 million; and Marketing Directions, Newport Beach, $11 million.

How big is the advertising agency business in Orange County? About 200 companies are listed, according to Jack Mealer (of Mealer & Emerson Advertising in Costa Mesa), who is a past president of the Orange County Ad Club. But that figure can be pared, he told *Orange County Businessweek* (8/3/87), to about 50 or fewer "large" agencies (those that have been in business more than a year and employ three or more people, and place advertising fairly frequently) when the one-person operations are subtracted. Although well distributed throughout Orange County's 27 incorporated cities, a heavy concentration of ad organizations is located near the John Wayne Airport.

As people break away from established firms to start their own companies, Orange County's communications field gains experienced promotional and marketing talent, and local businesspeople no longer believe that they have to go to Los Angeles to get the creative professionalism they need. Louise Michaels, of Clark, Meyer, Charters & Howell, in Huntington Beach, told *Orange County Businessweek* (8/3/87), "Not only are we holding our own against Los Angeles agencies, but in some cases we're taking business from their area."

A relatively new aspect of marketing communications that until recently has been virtually ignored is the growing Hispanic consumer market. Spanish-speaking Americans number about 18 million, of which over 324,000 live in Orange County, according to updated 1980 census figures.

Tapping into the Hispanic market, "has been a long time coming," said Andre Sullivan, creative director of Mendoza, Dillon y Asociados, an eight-year-old Newport Beach advertising company that claims to be the largest of its kind in the U.S., with 1986 revenues of $6 million on client billings of $40 million (OCB 8/3/87).

Although outside advertising agencies and law firms may be having trouble moving into Orange County and sharing some of its growth, such is not the case with the accounting concerns.

Numerous accounting establishments, from small independents to major companies, keep the "bottom line" straight for Orange County's

J.W. Robinson's is one of the many stores that make up the Mission Viejo Mall. Photo by John Sanford

$50-billion-dollar economy. They include 10 of the nation's 15 largest: Peat Marwick Main & Company (Peat Marwick merged with KMG Main Hurdman in April 1987); Arthur Andersen & Company; Deloitte, Haskins & Sells; Arthur Young & Company; Ernst & Whinney; Price Waterhouse, Coopers & Lybrand; Laventhol & Horwath; Kenneth Leventhal & Company; and Touche Ross & Company.

Of the county's 24 largest accounting firms (based on the number of professional staff members), 18 companies are located in the Costa Mesa/Irvine/Newport Beach triangle, considered to be Orange County's primary professional services and financial district.

As the largest accounting firm in the area, Peat Marwick's history since 1975, says managing partner Ronald L. Merriman, represents a microcosm of Orange County's development. Merriman recalls:

In 1975 we had fewer than thirty-five people, and today we have about 280. We saw a lot of good things happening to the county at the time, and basically we fortified our office with people who, throughout their careers, have served entrepreneurial-type companies and who have in-depth experience in real estate, financial institutions, and complex tax situations—areas where Orange County has flourished in the last ten or twelve years.

Admittedly "high" on the area (which he calls a "living economy" because he is able to "live where I work and work where I live," compared to commuter cities like New York or Washington, D.C.), Merriman says that "what sets Orange County apart is its business core; its full-scope business community that twenty or thirty years ago maybe started up around a nice place to live, but today that is just an added dimension to the whole package."

Orange County's complete business community has grown to the point where it now includes a score of financial services, some of which, like venture capital funding, were non-existent during its formative years and virtually absent as recently as a decade ago, thus forcing the

ABOVE: The South Coast Plaza and the 405 Freeway are accented by the snowcapped Saddleback Mountains in the distance. Photo by Michele Burgess

RIGHT: Outdoor cafes and shops line this Orange County street. Photo by Mark E. Gibson

Peat Marwick's office in Costa Mesa features sleek modern styling. Photo (c) Bielenberg 1986

county's businesspeople to seek venture funds through urban centers like Los Angeles, San Francisco, Chicago, or New York.

However, encouraged by the county's intense developments in the high-tech and medical technology industries beginning in the late-1970s, industry watchers estimate that between 15 and 20 venture capital firms have headquarters or branch offices here.

Spawned by the area's medical technology industry, venture capital funds with equity interest are also increasing for the makers of pharmaceuticals, diagnostic equipment, biotechnology products, and health-care services. "There's a hotbed of med-tech activity in Orange County and San Diego," said Walt Kortschak (OCB 7/27/87), an associate with the Newport Beach-based Crosspoint Venture Partners, and "a perception that you can serve both areas by being situated in Newport Beach."

It is a perception that Michael A. Henos agrees with. Henos is a venture capitalist with Investors in Industry, known as 3i. Headquartered in the United Kingdom, 3i began its U.S. investments in 1980 from an office in Boston, Massachusetts.

ABOVE: Biomatrix in the Carnegie Centre awaits the start of another business day. Photo by Jim Mendenhall

FACING PAGE: Dining alfresco has never been more elegant. Photo by Jim Mendenhall

Realizing substantial successes in its initial ventures, the company was motivated to make a broader commitment to U.S. business in 1983 and, subsequently, to select Orange County as its West Coast base of operations. Explaining that 3i's primary interests are in the health care and electronics fields, Henos says that "Southern California offers a plethora of opportunities for the strongest growth in our specialized areas. Orange County's position between Los Angeles and San Diego contributed to 3i's decision makers' choice of location."

As part of a 1987 briefing on Orange County's economy for members of the international consular corps, Fred M. Haney (3i's managing partner at the Newport Beach office), stated that in 1983 the county's six venture capital firms had access to about $50 million worth of venture capital. By 1987 the number of firms with headquarters or branch offices in the county had tripled, and the combined amount of venture capital they had access to was "about $1.5 billion," Haney said (OCB 7/27/87). "That's quite a change—thirty times expansion in four years."

What forces does Haney see shaping the venture capital industry, and how do they affect Orange County?

Traditional technology industries (high-tech electronics, semiconductors, and segments of the computer industry) have been in recession, Haney told the consular corps, and international competition has compounded the situation. Entrepreneurs and investors have been forced to look for smaller niche markets where they can add much more value and create a stronger competitive position.

Haney contends that just as the Silicon Valley produced a venture capital community that provided for the needs of its semiconductor and computer industries, so will Orange County evolve "a venture capital industry that meets the needs of start-up medical and health care companies and the systems and software companies that are the users and appliers of core computer technologies" (OCB 7/27/87).

Walter Cruttenden, one of Orange County's earliest entrants into investment banking and venture capital funding, believes that more demand for investment banking services is in the offing because the regional economy is growing faster than that of the rest of the nation. "Even with some of our problems, like transportation and high housing costs," Cruttenden declares, "I'm bullish on Orange County's future. I think we have another five or ten years of reasonable growth, and then we'll probably be in line with the rest of the nation."

Cruttenden organized Cruttenden & Company in 1977 to handle investment banking transactions. He followed that in 1983 with the formation of the Irvine Technology Fund (which, he says, "is just a little pocket to make some direct investments into companies"), and in 1987, with partners Mark Van Mourick and Garfield Logan, he launched Optivest, "for the purpose of managing accounts for high net-worth individuals and smaller institutions that want personal service and money invested in growth situations."

Although Cruttenden & Company's main business is investment banking (acting as a broker and arranging transactions between investors and client companies), the company got caught up in the high-tech and medical technology growth of the 1970s and, between 1977 and 1987, raised $125 million in venture capital for 50 companies (three-quarters of them headquartered in Orange County).

According to the *Los Angeles Times* (6/7/87), Cruttenden aspires to becoming a regional firm in the tradition of Hambrecht & Quist or Montgomery Securities in northern California. In that respect, his company differs from Newport Beach-based Hagerty, Stewart & Associates, which prefers to remain small, said founder Kelly Hagerty, "because we want to know our clients, their wives and their kids" (LAT 6/7/87).

ABOVE: Fun-filled action can be found at Balboa Island. Photo by Mark E.Gibson

Following 21 years with Dean Witter Reynolds, and rising to vice president and manager of the firm's Santa Ana office by 1978, the *Times* said that Hagerty and one of his brokers pooled $100,000 to start their own firm, working with companies seeking venture capital or private placements of stock. Of the larger brokerages, Hagerty stated that "they just kept getting bigger and bigger, and I like to provide a more personalized service" (LAT 6/7/87).

The company opened in a 600-square-foot office, with 500 retail clients, and turned a profit of $78,000 the first year. Today, operating from a 4,000-square-foot office, Hagerty, Stewart & Associates' eight brokers serve 1,200 retail clients (about two-thirds of the company's business; the balance is generated from the corporate finance division). And, although Hagerty declined to say how much business the firm does now, he said that "revenues are growing at about 20 percent a year" (LAT 6/7/87).

Orange County has become the third-largest recipient of venture capital in the nation, behind the Silicon Valley and the Boston area, accord-

ing to Art Perrone, Jr., president of Geneva Business Services (LAT 5/3/87). "... It has been one of the leading counties in the U.S. in terms of initial public stock offerings by companies seeking a broader base of financing."

Not only is the area attractive to foreign investment, Perrone told the *Times*, but it "is also an incubator for new ideas and technology and is filled with hundreds of small businesses, the bulk of which are in the industries of tomorrow."

Helping to finance those industries, other venture capital firms with headquarters or branch offices in Orange County include: Marwit Capital Corporation, Security Pacific Capital, Enterprise Partners, First Interstate Ventures, Ventana Growth Funds, Southern California Capital Corporation, Security Pacific Capital Corporation, New West Ventures, Mountain Pacific Equities, Investments Orange Nassau, Dima Ventures, and Diehl & Company.

A large portion of these firms' funds are directed towards medical technology and health care companies, a situation that is enhanced by

Colorful lights reflect the excitement at the Balboa Fun Zone in Newport Beach. Photo by Michele Burgess

the growing prominence of the University of California/Irvine's medical research institution, which contributes to the human resources available to the industry, says Dick Allen (a former Caremark executive who left the home care corporation to form Dima Ventures). "In five to ten years, Orange County will be to med tech what Silicon Valley was to high tech several years ago" (OCB 7/27/87).

Moving from venture capital to other financial services, year-end reports stated that most of the county's 42 banks and 32 savings institutions enjoyed at least modest profits as total bank assets rose 21 percent, from $2.9 billion in 1985 to $3.5 billion in 1986, partly fueled by lower interest rates and a high volume of mortgages and refinancings. The new federal tax law was also viewed as a future boon to the lending industry as consumers began transferring their non-deductible credit card and other loan interest costs into home equity loans.

Chapman College's December 1986 economic review forecast an increase of 107 percent in eight years in Orange County's total bank deposits, from $8.4 billion in 1981 to $17.5 billion in 1987, placing the combined deposits in Los Angeles and Orange County on a par with the nation's number one money center, New York City.

Despite 1986 profits for some financial houses, however, others were not immune to industry-wide problems. A total of six county banks and savings and loan institutions failed during the year; a result, economists say, of loans associated with the oil and agriculture industries, and the county's rapid real estate expansion of the eighties.

The closures brought the county's total of failed financial organizations (since 1982) to eight banks, four savings and loans, and one thrift (approximately 20 percent of similar failures statewide). About 11 percent of California's financial institutions are located in Orange County.

Asian banks continue to broaden their visibility, based on the region's overall economic vitality and its collection of about 2,000 high-technology companies, and bank officials' belief in Orange County's ties with Pacific Rim countries. In 1986 seven Japanese banks, with total 1984 assets of $15.7 billion, claimed 39 branches in the county, many acquired through mergers with local banks (OCR 1/19/86). They include: California First (since 1975, a Bank of Tokyo subsidiary); Bank of California (1984); Sumitomo (1966); Mitsui Manufacturers (1981); Golden State Sanwa (1978); Mitsubishi (1976); and Tokai (1975).

Whether banks, law offices, accounting firms, or a multitude of other Orange County companies, many are relying on placement services to provide them with personnel, and temporary workers are more in demand than permanent employees. Tustin-based Abigail Abbott, for example, placed 10,000 temporaries in 1986, compared to 2,500 full-time placements, says founder-owner Louise Pomeroy. And Anaheim-based Volt Temporary Services "places an average of 12,000 people a month through its four Orange County offices, up 24 percent from last year," said area manager Carol Sneed (OCB 2/16/87). "I can't see anything that indicates it will slow."

As Orange County's economy evolved from agriculture to manufacturing to high technology to services, the demand for part-time employees increased (they are also referred to as independents, freelancers, consultants, temporaries, contract or contingency workers, and disposable employees).

The largest among Orange County's 40-plus temporary placement

FACING PAGE: The South Coast Metro Center features this Southern California habitat. Photo by John Sanford

firms include: Abigail Abbott, Kelly Services, Manpower, Inc., Norrell Services, Remedy Temporary, Temp Associates, Thomas Temporaries, and Volt Temporary Services.

Whereas 20 years ago temporary personnel were used to fill in for an ill or vacationing employee, today they are being used more as a managing tool, says Ellen Rufe, Volt's Orange County manager of public relations. "Employers are planning ahead for part-time workers to help with peak periods and special projects. They aren't waiting until the crunch comes before calling us."

As the ranks of temporaries swell, so do the categories. Certain industries have always used a large number of temporary workers: retail, farming, food processing, secretarial, and nursing, for example. Those segments still make up a large portion of employer requests, but with the restructuring of some businesses to meet increased competition and the rapid technological changes that render some job tasks obsolete while creating new ones, Rufe says that more companies are requesting people with skills in word processing, computer technology, and telemarketing.

Abigail Abbott's Pomeroy (who admits that she never learned to type) agrees that technology has added a significant dimension to the sort of personnel that companies request. "Eighty percent of the county's businesses are on computers," she says, "and the demand now is for temporaries who know how to operate personal computers and who can handle financial data and spreadsheets. Fifty percent of our job orders for secretaries ask for word processing and data base management experience."

Pomeroy founded Abigail Abbott in 1970 as a permanent-personnel agency. Later, sensing the growing demand for part-time help, she

Gandhi serves Indian cuisine at the South Coast Plaza Village in Santa Ana. Photo by Yana Bridle

Newport Beach diners enjoy puttin' on the Ritz. Photo by Yana Bridle

started Abigail Abbott Temporaries in 1975. Temporaries now account for 50 percent of the company's business. Pomeroy estimated 1987 revenues at $20 million.

Discussing possible trends for employment services during the 1990s, Pomeroy affirms that specialized skills in professions like banking, insurance, accounting, legal, and health care will continue to grow, and, given Orange County's diverse economy and the impact of international trade, she also sees a greater need arising for bilingual services. As a result—following the same intuition that led to the opening of Abigail Abbott's temporaries division—the company has started recruiting people with linguistic abilities to fill job orders.

Pomeroy also foresees "tapping the resources of our senior citizens and the handicapped, because the declining birth rate will affect the labor force. Overall, I'd say we have a bright future."

Like its economic counterparts outlined in Chapter 3, the services industry has augmented the county's growth, and it now ranks, economically, as California's second-largest county. Displaying an element of entrepreneurial spirit and professional panache that deserves the term "first class," these economic cornerstones provide excellent examples that further contribute to Orange Countians' vision of a world-class image, the subject of the next chapter.

WORLD-CLASS IMAGE

ABOUT TWENTY-FIVE YEARS AGO THINGS JUST STARTED TO COME TOGETHER FOR US. I DON'T THINK ANYONE ENVISIONED THEN THAT ORANGE COUNTY WOULD BECOME A WORLD-CLASS COMMUNITY.

—LUCIEN D. TRUHILL, ORANGE COUNTY CHAMBER OF COMMERCE

No longer considered a newly emerging economic and social entity, and not yet a fully developed one, Orange County is in the process of refining three decades of growth activity.

It is probably true that "back then" no one envisioned the scope of the county's development, or the impact it would have on California's economy, or the fact that some innovative government and social programs would influence other U.S. cities' officials, or that Orange County would play a significant role on the world-trade stage.

Neither would anyone have suspected years ago that Orange County's school systems—public and private, from kindergarten through higher education—would be lauded as some of the best in the nation; nor that its master-planned communities would be models for city planners elsewhere.

To outsiders, such broad-scale accomplishments are difficult to understand. To Orange Countians, however, it is simply the way things are done, with passion and commitment, and a sincere sense of quality and professionalism.

The fact that Orange County as a whole qualifies as an economic entity—composed of 27 cities, in contrast to a region maintaining a single-city business core—adds a dimension to political and economic issues, and to subsequent compromises, that most other communities do not encounter.

"Our heritage has been a can-do attitude," says Robert C. Payton (vice

FACING PAGE: Pacific Savings Plaza in Costa Mesa greets its patrons with this majestic fountain.
Photo by Michele Burgess

president, public relations, of Basso & Associates). "One of our strengths is that we don't have a city core where the major business activity is centered; it's pretty diverse throughout the county. Everyone is interested in the county as a whole, yet also interested separately in the Santa Anas, Irvines, Oranges, San Clementes, and so on. *People* are our strength."

Economic diversification, according to Lucien D. Truhill (president and chief executive officer of the 75-year-old Orange County Chamber of Commerce), "is one of the things that helps make us a world-class economy. I don't know of another place in the U.S. that has the economic balance we have. If one industry or business sector is down we have five, six, or ten other sectors coming up strong."

Truhill can recall vividly when Orange County's economy was not so well-balanced. An experienced certified industrial developer, he was brought into the chamber in 1962 to help direct the county's economic development. "Such industry as we had," he says, "was concentrated in aerospace, which went through a considerable shakedown in 1972. Although five years earlier we had started a program to diversify, and it was beginning to have some impetus, we weren't prepared for the situation in the aerospace industry."

Today, in view of Orange County's $50-billion economy and low unemployment rate (which for several years has floated between 3.5 percent and 4.5 percent, compared to twice-and-thrice that rate elsewhere), an attempt to visualize the critical economic consequences attendant on the l970s' aerospace shakeout strains the imagination. Says Truhill, "People don't realize it, but Orange County experienced some real hardship then and we were front-page news as one of the major unemployment areas in the entire nation."

But the old adage, "Class will tell," is aptly born out in the preceding

FACING PAGE, TOP: Bicyclists pedal along the bike path in Huntington Beach Park. Photo by John Sanford

FACING PAGE, BOTTOM: The student union at Cal State Fullerton is a place to talk and relax. Courtesy, Cal State Fullerton

BELOW: Fullerton High School is just one of the facilities in Orange County devoted to the furthering of education. Photo by Mark E. Gibson

chapters describing Orange County's economic, social, and cultural achievements.

Furthermore, there is a perennial degree of excellence, pride, and professionalism underscoring Orange Countians' efforts to build and sustain the quality of life that attracted them to the county in the first place.

Darrell E. Metzger, president of Orange County Centennial, Inc. (OCCI) says that educating local citizens, as well as a larger audience, of the county's historical roots and its present attributes and future potential, "is part of our mission statement."

Formerly a vice president at Management Resources in Tustin, Metzger, assisted by a 17-member board of trustees and various committees, comes well equipped to handle the details of Orange County's year-long centennial celebration. He spent 10 years with the Walt Disney Company (where he developed plans for Tokyo Disneyland), and was involved with the hiring and training of paid and volunteer staff for the 1984 Los Angeles Olympic Organizing Committee; two years later he managed the operational plan for Expo '86 in Vancouver, British Columbia.

The individual who got everyone excited about the centennial was Frank Ducey, a longstanding member of the Orange County Chamber of Commerce, which was designated by the county board of supervisors as the official body responsible for organizing the celebration.

Commencing on August 1, 1988, and ending on the county's 100th birthday on August 1, 1989, "the event is more than just a party," Metzger says. "It's an attempt to create an awareness of, and an appreciation for, the entrepreneurial spirit that has brought Orange County so far."

In addition to OCCI's efforts to organize an unforgettable centennial observance, Metzger emphasizes that "it will help to establish our identity and credibility, not just regionally, but nationally, and, to some ex-

tent, internationally. We're going to let the world know where Orange County is, what it is, and what it has to offer, so we don't have to describe it anymore as 'south of Los Angeles.'"

Funded privately by corporate donations, sponsorships, and in-kind contributions, the 12-month celebration will focus on participation by all 27 cities, and will include about 100 artistic, educational, and historical programs, as well as other special events, like baseball's sixtieth Major League All-Star Game, scheduled to be played at Anaheim Stadium in July 1989.

In August 1989, the celebrating will be over, but the memory will linger on. "We have created a living, continuous memorial in the form of a scholarship foundation," Metzger says proudly. "It's our legacy, what we want the centennial to be remembered for."

With contributions, profits from some of the activities, and anticipated perpetual funding sources, "it should be a substantial scholarship fund," Metzger states. "Rather than building monuments and dedicating something in bricks and mortar, we're really putting that money into the future, into our young people who will be the leaders and business-people of Orange County."

While centennial activities will undoubtedly extend Orange County's recognition factor and enhance its image (and, many hope, dispel the notion that Orange County exists only as a surf and shopping mall culture, as one publication stated), it must be noted that other, sometimes subtle, features also contribute to an image that places Orange County in a world-class category—that enviable position of effecting influence well beyond its borders.

The county's widespread reputation as a high technology and re-

FACING PAGE: Beachgoers enjoy a sunset at Corona del Mar. Photo by John Sanford

LEFT: Fans pack Anaheim Stadium. Photo by Jim Mendenhall

search center, for example, and its expanding importance in the world of international trade, have already been discussed in previous chapters, along with some of the area's highly visible, right-on-the-surface image enhancers; to name only a few: Irvine Spectrum, the 2,200-acre research and business complex; the $73-million, privately funded Orange County Performing Arts Center; South Coast Repertory Theatre, one of the nation's leading lights in American theatre; the World Trade Center; the Irvine Business Complex/John Wayne Airport area; and South Coast Plaza, the nationally known retail center whose 1987 projected annual sales totaled more than downtown San Francisco's.

Digging beneath the surface, however, for that *world class* measure, one finds examples as varied as the people who offer them, depending on the context of their experience.

Like "smart" buildings (for example, AT&T's offices in Irvine Spectrum, high rises in MacArthur Court and Jamboree Center, or Bergen Brunswig's corporate headquarters in the City of Orange). Frank L. Smith, an independent economic development consultant, says that these buildings are so technologically advanced that everything from energy efficient environments to security systems, and access to major telecommunications networks, are all linked to centralized computers, thus providing a high level of under-one-roof technological sophistication, which is a definite plus in today's rapidly expanding and increasingly competitive national and international markets.

For Leon Schwartz, vice chancellor of the university's Administration Business Services and director of the UCI Medical Center (located in Orange), the county's ability to project an image of leadership means that "the medical center's Burn Unit and Neonatal Center have to be

FACING PAGE: Boats head out to
the high seas from Dana Point Harbor. Photo by Jim Mendenhall

on anybody's list as the best of their kind in California."

Similarly, in the area of health care services, Childrens Hospital of Orange County is regarded as the regional center for the treatment of children with unusual and highly complicated medical conditions.

From a political perspective, Supervisor Roger R. Stanton (who represents the first district on the Orange County Board of Supervisors, and who served as the board's chairman during 1983 and 1987) says, "If you want something 'world class', you're talking to a politician, so my orientation concerning what's world class in Orange County revolves around how well we're doing in local government."

Based on Stanton's observations and meetings with city officials in other parts of the nation, he says Orange County's government is "outstanding by comparison. We have a reputation as a first-class act in terms of innovativeness, the type of programs that we pursue, and the quality of personnel we hire."

Referring to two programs "that are being looked at nationwide," Stanton recalls that in the early 1980s, with the full realization of an influx of Indochinese refugees throughout the nation, "Orange County's response was to set up a network, coordinated by a project organization team, [whose purpose was] to correlate procedures between private organizations, school districts, and social service agencies, and to do a quick study on how to best help assimilate these folks into the community."

The outline for that program, Stanton explains, "was based on an aerospace model of project management, where you're presented with unusual circumstances in an unusual environment and you need to take quick action."

To Orange County's credit, Stanton adds, "President Reagan's ambassador for refugee affairs took particular note of our efforts [because] we avoided all of the usual urban problems associated with a rapid influx of refugees, and today have a very placid environment and a very productive Vietnamese community."

Stanton's second example of an innovative program that has attracted outside attention originated in the Orange County District Attorney's office, "and it's one that I'm very proud of," he says.

In 1982, in unison with our social services agency, a totally unique early detection and prevention system directed at welfare fraud was devised, and it has saved this county millions and millions of dollars in AFDC [Aid to Families with Dependent Children] money, which the county administers for the federal and state governments. The program has been noted with great interest and I have had many visitors from California, as well as officials from Alaska, discuss it with me, and the welfare fraud director from New York City came out to see what we were doing.

Along the line of social structures and networks, the Orange County Chamber of Commerce's Truhill maintains there is "a framework—an infrastructure—of volunteerism that hasn't yet been fully recognized as one of our greatest strengths. When people talk of infrastructure," Truhill says,

they're usually thinking of roads and freeways, or sewer systems and utilities, but it's more than that. In addition to the business infrastruc-

GALER

ture, like the Orange County Chamber and the cities' chambers of commerce, the Merchants and Manufacturers, and the Industrial League, among others, there's another one that goes deeper than that. I'm talking about the social agencies that are here: United Way, Red Cross, Salvation Army—but even deeper than that, for example, the Crittenton Home and Orangewood [both involved in children's services].

Volunteerism is pretty strong here, and long before the word[s] public and private partnership [were] coined, we were using [them]. When the Vietnam refugees started coming in, for example, we weren't ready for them in the sense that we were prepared, but we were ready automatically, because of this strong sociological framework... We're beginning to draw together and work with the social, public, governmental, and business infrastructures.

It is this drawing together of Orange County's various elements—woven into an integrated, textured economy, with a social consciousness and a sufficiently pleasing lifestyle—that is gradually creating an image less often derided by outsiders for its lack of culture, its conservative politics, and its cookie-cutter houses.

Despite misconceptions and a lingering fuzziness nationally about what and where Orange County is, "it is developing what appears to be an increasingly strong local identity," Lou Weiss (president of the Newport Beach-based American Marketing Services) told the *Orange County Register* (6/28/87).

Polling adults in Los Angeles and Orange counties, as well as opinion leaders in California and the nation, the *Register* found that nine out of ten Orange Countians think positively about their county, and that only one in ten Los Angeles residents had a negative view of the former suburb. The opinion sampling also revealed that Los Angelenos recognize Orange County as a separate metropolitan area.

The county's sophistication and status in the state caught Leon Schwartz (UCI Medical Center's director) by surprise. A relative newcomer to the county from the East Coast (where he was the director of administration at the National Institutes of Health in Washington, D.C.), Schwartz offers an "outsider's observation" that he "had no concept, for example, of the importance of the University of California [system,] or what it meant to the state. I knew that nationally it was a highly regarded institution, but I didn't know how important it is in the state legislature."

And, says Schwartz, "I *completely* underestimated the importance of UC Irvine within Orange County. The fact there is a University of California presence here is just very, very important."

In making this "rather subtle point," Schwartz thinks that "people might not fully appreciate what I'm saying. Those who have lived here all their life probably take it for granted that the University of California is good."

That academic "goodness," in relation to the world-class components that distinguish Orange County from other regions, Schwartz continues, "provides it with opportunities that only about 100 other communities in the nation possess: having both a medical school and a medical facility within its borders. Only about 50 of those schools would think of themselves as a medical research center. We fit into that category."

FACING PAGE: This graceful sculpture adorns the Imperial Bank plaza on Town Center Drive in Costa Mesa. Photo by John Sanford

Fifty percent of UCI's research originates in the College of Medicine. Of that, Schwartz notes, about 75 percent (including the school of biosciences), is related to research in the biological sciences.

What is the proposed goal for UCI Medical Center?

To become known as the "university hospital of Orange County," Schwartz replies, and to gain a reputation as a major research center in the tradition of UCLA or UC Berkeley. Towards that end, approximately $40 million has recently been allocated by the state legislature for various improvements and construction projects, including state-of-the-art intensive care and psychiatric units; two private practice facilities, one at the medical center in Orange and the other on the UCI campus; and a cancer center, which is scheduled for completion in 1989.

(Besides UCI Medical Center's cancer facility, Orange County residents will see, over the next several years, the construction of an outpatient cancer division at Hoag Memorial Hospital Presbyterian in Newport Beach, and the completion of a cancer center at St. Joseph Hospital in Orange.)

The 1,500-acre UCI campus, which sprawls in the foothills of the Santa Ana Mountains and graduated its first class in 1965, has already attained national recognition for its creative writing program, which ranks with that of the University of Iowa, and for its research expertise, which includes study of sleep disorders, laser surgery, genetic engineering, burn treatments, cardiovascular surgery, brain and spinal cord rehabilitation, and studies of motion sickness.

As one of the nation's top 50 research universities (a position strengthened by the presence of the National Academy of Sciences, which allows the university faculty the opportunity to interact with visitors from around the world), UCI is also acclaimed for breakthroughs in elementary particle physics, psychobiology, atmospheric chemistry, and literary criticism.

The university's enrollment has climbed along with its stature. In l965, 1,589 students crisscrossed the campus, which was still little more than a free-roaming habitat for deer, rabbits, and other assorted small animals. By l987, in an environment of rapidly developing academic facil-

The University of California, Irvine campus graduated its first class in 1965. It boasts a major medical hospital and teaching facility. Over 60 percent of its alumni reside in Orange County. Photo by Mark E. Gibson

Assembly of Collegiate Schools of Business (AACSB), an endorsement that can be used as a marketing tool to recruit faculty and enroll more students.

The AACSB accreditation places the graduate school in the same league as the management schools at the University of Southern California, California State/Long Beach, San Diego State, and UC Los Angeles.

Moving from UC Irvine to the City of Orange's Chapman College, a small private school with about one-seventh the regular student body (2,100 full-time students in 1987 versus UCI's 15,000), we find an institution that is "really looking to the shrinking world, and sensitive to the fact that our students are going to deal more and more with international issues," says Jerry Derloshon, Chapman's director of public relations. "Our outreach programs extend well beyond U.S. boundaries."

A case in point: the 52 regional education centers (REC) around the world that more than double Chapman's student enrollment. The REC program was started "about twenty-seven years ago at the El Toro Marine Base," Derloshon says, "when the college was the first to respond to an invitation by the Marine Corps to offer degree courses to military personnel."

Another Chapman "first" that may develop into a long-term, far-reaching success, and which students may beneficially adapt to their daily lives in a shrinking world, is the required freshman seminar focusing on analytical thinking, which was introduced in fall 1987. The subject of war and peace initiated the program.

Recognizing (with other schools nationwide) that liberal arts studies have suffered, and that students over the years have been abandoning humanities courses to pursue only curriculums pertaining to their career orientation, Chapman College—which aims to become one of the nation's top liberal arts schools—decided to subtly "force" entering freshman to learn to examine a subject from many perspectives. It may be the first college course in Southern California to bring an entire freshman class together to study just one subject.

Through a variety of disciplines (language, biology, music, history, political science, and film, among others), the seminar will help to build the process of sophisticated, flexible thinking, Derloshon says. "Students will learn to examine, debate, and write, and then be able to relate those analytical skills to other areas of their lives."

It is "especially perplexing," said a *Los Angeles Times* editorial (7/23/87), "that too often there is not enough analytical thinking where you would most expect to find it—on college campuses."

The *Times* found it encouraging that some schools had started to think about that, and that Chapman College had actually implemented an innovative course to teach critical reasoning.

Innovation, vision, and planning for the future are the overriding themes that direct Orange County's march into the twenty-first century. Those characteristics, coupled with a "high energy output," Derloshon believes, "are Orange Countians' way of responding to and creating change, rather than merely reacting to change."

It is that vital energy, and Orange Countians' ability to seize ideas and effectively transform them into impressive examples, that account for Orange County becoming a world-class community.

AT THE HELM

WHEN COMPARED TO SOME OTHERS AROUND THE NATION, ORANGE COUNTY'S LOCAL GOVERNMENT IS OUTSTANDING.

—ROGER R. STANTON, ORANGE COUNTY BOARD OF SUPERVISORS, FIRST DISTRICT

It is not by happenstance that a region grows into a thriving, vital, and rich—and enriching—community. Such economic, social, and cultural achievements as discussed in the preceding chapters are the result of concentrated efforts by the majority of Orange Countians, be they executives, entrepreneurs, builders, pioneers, or regular folks.

Over 2 million people work, live, and play in Orange County, and 34 million more visit each year. Business organizations, like the local chambers of commerce, the Orange County Chamber of Commerce, and the Industrial League of Orange County, regularly field queries from individuals and companies alike who are interested in knowing more about this southern California "phenomenon." Orange Countians must be doing *something* right.

The right something is more than just broad-range activity by energetic can-doers: people who display, through vision, initiative, and resourcefulness, an uncommon amount of enterprising spirit. It also signifies a core of conscientious leadership and management at the county and city government levels, and from the social and business communities.

More than that, however, Orange Countians in general evince a strong awareness about their county and its development, and they actively and vocally demonstrate that they intend to be counted as participants in the shaping of its future, whether that means (among other issues) working diligently to secure private funds for the construction of the

FACING PAGE: Orange County hugs the coast of the blue Pacific. Photo by Jeff Marks

The lofty *Pilgrim* takes part in a tall ships race. Photo by Chris Bryant

$73-million Orange County Performing Arts Center; taking sides on the subject of growth; or defeating Proposition A, a 1984 ballot initiative that asked voters to raise the sales tax from 6 percent to 7 percent, with the additional penny allotted to highway and transit improvements over a 15-year period.

Inevitably, there are social and urban concerns that need to be addressed in California's third-largest county.

Traffic congestion needs no introduction, says Robert Payton, vice president, public relations, of Basso & Associates. "And health care, toxic wastes, and sufficient water are issues coming up that can really impact us severely if we don't wise up."

In addition, the county's social, health, and other services, Payton continues, "are being impacted very dramatically by immigrants from around the world. It's an expensive endeavor. At the same time, cities are running out of money to deal with their needs because of growth and the tax base. It's not an easy problem."

Are Orange Countians wising up and addressing these issues?

"I think so, with the benefit of good leadership and good, responsible people throughout the county," Payton replies.

We have a good basis to grow on and an excellent system of government, and that reflects well on changes in the county. I have the utmost confidence in all five members of the Board of Supervisors, as well as in the majority of local leadership. But it's not going to get any easier as the challenges become greater.

ABOVE: Surf's up at Seal Beach.
Photo by Mark E. Gibson

ABOVE LEFT: Bathers wade in at
this Balboa beach. Photo by Mark
E. Gibson

A significant characteristic of good local government (the term covers county and city administrations) that stands in contrast to other parts of the nation, according to First District Supervisor Roger R. Stanton, is "the lack of patronage and partisanship in elective offices."

As a participant in the Program for Senior Executives in State and Local Government (held in the summer of 1985 at the John F. Kennedy School of Government at Harvard University) Stanton returned to Orange County "with a great appreciation for the fact that our technical people—bridge inspectors, planners, engineers, and so forth—are hired on the strength of their professional resumes, not on the basis of who they supported or worked for during an election."

Compared to local governments on the East Coast, in the Midwest, and to some extent in the South, Stanton says, "California, and particularly southern California, probably has the best reputation for professionalism. This leads to a higher quality of government service product, as opposed to some other parts of the country where, when new people are elected, sometimes whole departments are cleaned out and new people come in."

The absence of the patronage process in Orange County government is a positive feature, Stanton adds, "that most folks who haven't left the area don't know about. But people who have migrated here from other parts of the U.S. can appreciate it."

While agreeing that there is "no question about how good local government is," Second District Supervisor Harriett M. Wieder states there is definitely room for improvement: "We need a broader commitment of working together. The left hand doesn't know what the right hand is doing. I think our problems demonstrate that."

To explore ways for the county agencies and the 27 city governments to coordinate efforts in solving problems of a regional nature, Wieder introduced a resolution (in 1987 and forwarded to all the city councils

The business of city life is conducted at Huntington Beach City Hall. Photo by Jim Mendenhall

for evaluation) that calls for the establishment of a countywide governing council, to achieve, she says, "an equitable means of balancing regional needs with each city's governing control . . . We have overriding [regional] concerns that are a part of the inheritance of our growth from a rural to an urban metropolis."

Although an attempt was made in the mid-1970s to organize a county government body, the idea did not take root. However, in the ensuing years, Wieder claims, "the need for one has increased and it's been brought into sharper focus."

A major advantage that would stem from the establishment of a county governing council, she says, would be additional funding for regional programs. The regulatory body would be identified by the federal government as a metropolitan planning organization, thus making the county eligible for funds to finance the area's coordinated projects.

As she began her elected third term in 1987, Wieder noted that although Orange County's outstanding growth has produced jobs and reflects a healthy economy, "traffic is bad and getting worse. Our air quality is not as good as it should be, and we are facing critical problems in the disposal of hazardous wastes. Also, unless we act soon, we could be facing severe water shortages within the next few years" (BOC 1/87).

Orange Countians need to manage the growth without discouraging it, Wieder stresses, "but this is *not* something that government can—or should—do in a vacuum."

Citing land use as just one example of a civic concern that extends beyond a city's borders, Wieder says, "Whatever one city does with respect to land-use planning can affect the whole county, and that reality,

This Lake Forrest truck dealer has a make and model for every taste.
Photo by Jim Mendenhall

You've gotta slug it out, literally, almost intersection by intersection, driveway by driveway, from one end of the county to the other, and develop a plan coherent with all those cities, businesses, and property owners.

With the arrival of the Santa Ana Freeway in 1955, Orange County's assets—balmy climate, ocean playground, jobs, space, Disneyland (which had just opened), and a relaxed lifestyle—called out to the world and thousands responded.

Eight more freeways and numerous multilane surface streets intersected the county in the next three decades, making it approachable from all directions. No one then could have predicted the astronomical growth that would take place, first through in-migration but now self-generated as Orange County's birth rate exceeds, by nearly three times, the rate of deaths.

How bad is traffic congestion in Orange County?

So bad that residents spend a median of almost two and a half hours a day on the road, according to a special report by the *Orange County Register* (11/30/86).

So bad that residents rank traffic problems above crime and high housing costs; and so bad, the report said, that a 19-mile stretch of the San Diego Freeway (Interstate 405) takes over 45 minutes to drive during rush hour, a trip more than twice as long as it was six years ago.

Orange County records more than 12,000 cars per freeway mile, the highest ratio of any county in California, and more than three times the statewide average, the *Register* said. The county also has 11,000 licensed drivers per freeway mile, again more than three times the statewide average.

The freeway speeds during rush hours average between 35 and 45 miles per hour, and will probably drop to half that by the year 2000, if the forecasts by the California Department of Transportation hold true.

Ironically, the very term "rush hour" has lost its meaning, as eight-to-ten-hour stretches of congestion inch along some county freeways,

Canoes are neatly lined up at the Balboa Yacht Club. Photo by Yana Bridle

like the Santa Ana (Interstate 5) and the Costa Mesa/Newport (State 55), for a major portion of the commuters' day.

Displaying a sense of humor that underscores reality, "and gets some people mad at me," OCTC's Oftelie says, "the traffic is better today than it will *ever* be again."

But, he is quick to point out, "We can significantly retard the deterioration of our transportation system, and we have and we are. But if we don't take significant steps—take destiny into our own hands and take responsibility for the problem—transportation will never be as good as it is today."

When Orange County voters overwhelmingly defeated Proposition A in 1984, "we learned something," Oftelie says. "People don't think we're spending transportation funds wisely. They clearly believe that we can do a better job with the funds available, and until we demonstrate we can, they aren't going to give us any more money."

Oftelie, though optimistic that "we can catch up a lot," acknowledges that even as new procedures are being implemented to improve the system, "it may fall further behind, because developing and constructing an effective transportation system is a lengthy and expensive process. The environmental requirements alone are enormous in terms of time, design, and manpower."

Furthermore, no matter what positive steps are taken, "the bottom line is that we need significant additional money," Oftelie says.

I'm not minimizing the good things we've done to improve transportation. Adding carpool lanes, building toll roads, staggering work hours, ridesharing, and creating the largest developers fees program in the U.S.

are all positive steps. But the cumulative weight of those steps won't turn our transportation system around without some substantial funding.

In the forefront of current traffic solutions is the toll road concept, which, according to Oftelie, has not been used in the state since the mid-nineteenth century Gold Rush days, although some private toll roads exist, like the scenic 17-mile drive in Carmel, in northern California.

A legislative bill to allow construction in Orange County of California's first public toll roads, under the authorship of California Senator John Seymour (R., Anaheim), was passed without debate by the Senate in September 1987, and signed into law by Governor George Deukmejian, who (although, reportedly, not keen on toll roads) recognized complaints by the county's business leaders that the California Department of Transportation (Caltrans) has a poor record of completing Orange County's freeway projects (OCR 9/12/87).

The bill (which will expire after the highway construction is completed) allows the county to implement toll facilities on three new planned highways: the Eastern Corridor, the Foothill Corridor, and the San Joaquin Hills Transportation Corridor, which would ease traffic on the Santa Ana, San Diego, and Costa Mesa/Newport freeways, and link south Orange County with thoroughfares in the north and west. The design, financing, and construction of the roadways is the responsibility of the Transportation Corridor Agencies, a joint-powers body consisting of representatives from the county and cities.

Construction is not expected on the Eastern and Foothill freeways until the mid-1990s. The San Joaquin Hills Corridor, however, which is the furthest along in the planning process, could be under construction by 1991 and open by late 1993. It was approved by the OCTC in October 1987, based on recommendations by a 15-member citizens panel, which also recommended that the county seek amendments to earlier federal toll road legislation that would allow federal money to be used for the planned Eastern and Foothill corridors, under the theory that the three highways will be part of one transportation system.

The passage of the Federal Highway Act named six states and Orange County as sites for an experimental toll road program, making the county eligible to receive 35 percent of its funding through the federal government. Developers fees are expected to finance 50 percent of the construction in South County, leaving only 15 percent of the cost to be collected by tolls.

When Senator Daniel P. Moynihan (D., New York) announced the states eligible for funding, Oftelie recalls, "he quipped that he didn't think Orange County would settle for statehood and was thinking of becoming a sovereign nation of its own. And there's some truth to that, when you consider we're one of only seven areas in the U.S. to be designated for federal toll road funding."

A speedboat cuts through the deep blue sea. Photo by Jim Mendenhall

Facing reductions in state and federal funds, as well as restrictions on the ability of counties to increase taxes for road-building programs, Orange County officials and business leaders began to investigate other ways to solve the transportation problem and to raise revenue for road construction and improvements.

An essential linchpin was their successful campaign to establish a California Department of Transportation district office in Orange County. Keith McKean, a veteran Caltrans engineer and administrator, took over as the director of the newly created Orange County district in July 1987.

Separating the county from the jurisdiction of the Los Angeles Caltrans office, officials said, was necessary to ensure that Orange County receives its fair share of state funds and resources, and to prevent proposed transportation projects from falling further behind schedule.

County leaders, in the vanguard with another plan to accommodate growth and ease transportation problems, promoted the contracting of agreements with developers for the construction of new roads; a move particularly applicable to South County, which is already taking the brunt of growth that will extend well into the twenty-first century.

To date, California is the only state that allows city or county governments to negotiate agreements with developers. Many Orange County builders endorsed the idea and, with county officials, even lobbied city councils for the enactment of developers fees in their cities.

Speaking out in favor of greater involvement by the building industry, William Lyon (chairman of the board and chief executive officer of the Newport Beach-based William Lyon Company, the state's largest homebuilder) said that growth and transportation issues will not be solved by the local, state, or federal government, but by the building industry itself.

"I know I'm talking heresy," Lyon told the Orange County chapter of the Building Industry Association (OCR 1/7/87), "[but] developers need to tax themselves to build Orange County's roads, or residents will restrict building and drive up home prices."

Referring (in the *Register* article) to the county as a Disneyland for grownups, because the real estate opportunities are unmatched in the nation, Lyon said that growth cannot be stopped: "I'm telling you, the Indians are coming over the hill. People want to live in Orange County."

Historically, developers agreements were first used by the Irvine Company, in the early 1980s, when road improvements were linked to building projects around the John Wayne Airport area and southeast Irvine.

Over the years, in addition to road improvements surrounding major housing and commercial developments, some Orange County developers have also funded much-needed infrastructure like sewer and water systems, new schools, and parks.

Pacts between the county and developers

A woman and her dog watch the water flow through the penstocks at Trabuco Creek. Photo by John Sanford

New homes await the influx of
homebuyers in Orange County.
Photo by Jim Mendenhall

reached new heights in 1987, following more than a year of negotiations, when the Orange County Board of Supervisors approved the Foothill Circulation Phasing Plan.

The plan provides for the construction of 133 "lane miles" and the upgrading of intersections in South County. It carries a price tag of $235 million, which makes it one of the most expensive public works projects in county history, rivaling the $296-million expansion of John Wayne Airport.

The agreements require that the work be funded in advance, so that road building (which will feed into South County's three new freeways) can get underway before commercial projects and most of the new housing (approximately 87,000 units over several years) are constructed. This provision (which includes a 10-year guarantee to participating builders that future zoning changes will not affect their under-construction projects) signals a major change in how residential units are built in the county. Formerly, housing and road construction occurred together. If a developer actually constructed only a portion of the homes and left the balance until later, the roads remained unfinished until the rest of the units were built.

Orange Countians' productive energy, say many business leaders, is being squandered on congested freeways, a condition exacerbated by two facts: People living outside the county's borders are taking advantage of its job opportunities, and Orange Countians are seeking more affordable housing in surrounding counties (in 1987 the median price for a new home was $190,000; for a resale home, $158,700); circumstances that put more vehicles on the freeways for longer periods of time.

Despite the imperative need for local government to study and resolve all the county's urban ills, the transportation problem looms as the number-one issue that needs the most immediate attention. The loss of time, personal and professional, observers say, cannot be measured, and could eventually curtail, drastically, Orange County's economic ef-

Aloe plants accent this seascape at Laguna Beach. Photo by Mick Roessler

ficiency.

Although not everyone welcomes developers agreements, the Orange County Board of Supervisors and other county officials, as well as various community groups, believe that significant regional public benefits are insured by the willingness of the county and the developers to enter into these contracts. Without them, they say, there is no realistic way of generating the large sums of money needed to effect road improvements and provide the necessary infrastructure.

Admittedly, the agreements may not be the "ideal world," Supervisor Roger R. Stanton told the *Los Angeles Times* (10/22/87), "but we have to deal with the real world."

Whispers of discontent with the county's growth began surfacing late in 1984 and in 1985, concerning traffic around the airport area and the Irvine Business Complex.

About the same time, Costa Mesa homeowners raised objections to certain aspects of C.J. Segerstrom & Sons' Crystal Court (an addition to South Coast Plaza mall, north of the San Diego Freeway, which was built after compromises between the company and nearby residents); followed by residents' opposition, in 1986, to construction of a proposed office-tower/hotel/art museum complex on the Segerstrom family's "Home Ranch" site in the same area.

In Newport Beach, voters in November 1986 defeated a ballot proposal that would have allowed furthur expansion of the Irvine Company's Newport Center/Fashion Island property.

From Seal Beach to San Clemente, one hears more frequently the collective voice of citizen concern, saying that development in the county has progressed too fast and too far.

But while real estate developers are being cast by some as the perpetrators of countywide congestion, other factors must also be considered: an aversion by Orange Countians to consider seriously a gasoline or sales tax increase, or to more widely adopt flexible work hours; or the reluctance of many to tailor their lifestyle to the realities connected with the county's growth and prosperity.

According to various reports, for example, the job market is growing rapidly, drawing commuters from Riverside, San Bernardino, and Los Angeles counties; one-passenger vehicles predominate over the use of ridesharing or public transportation. In addition, thousands of teenagers each year receive their driver's licenses, and the growth of families is increasing (one-third of the county's population is younger than age 18).

"The fault, dear Brutus, lies not in our stars but in ourselves," says Frank L. Smith, an independent economic development consultant. "If we do cause problems here in paradise it's because all of us have contributed, not just one person or entity. Some of us will have done it by not doing anything. Some of us will have done it by trying to do too much."

"If there wasn't a demand for housing and commercial construction," says Laguna Niguel-based developer Brandon Birtcher,

Choppers hover above the Tustin United States Marine Corps base. Photo by Jim Mendenhall

I wouldn't be here. I wouldn't have a job or be employing people—in other words, there wouldn't be a construction industry—if someone wasn't calling me up Monday through Friday asking for additional space for their company; or if a broker wasn't telephoning to say he's relocating a group from Cleveland.

Something that most people do not understand, Birtcher adds, "is that the development community is a *service* industry. It services growth, which is a natural phenomenon in a free, capitalistic society. You can't treat growth like a commodity, like it's a faucet that you can turn off and on when you want to."

Don Steffensen agrees. "Trying to stop growth is like playing with funny putty," says the Lusk Company's executive vice president.

Steffensen (president of the Building Industry Association of Southern California) believes that "a misconception exists that growth can be stopped. Natural expansion will occur. What we need are more efforts to equalize housing and jobs, and a lot more coordination on a regional basis."

Clearly, Orange Countians are caught between a rock and a hard place: How to temper the county's development and, at the same time, preserve a bountiful economy and an enviable lifestyle. "There has to be a limit on growth—maybe 2 percent," acknowledges Anthony Moiso (OCR 10/7/87), the president of the Rancho Santa Margarita Company, the state's second-largest landowner, behind the Irvine Company.

And, just as clearly, regardless of which side of the growth issue peo-

Lake Mission Viejo residents enjoy the opportunity to take their small boats for a leisurely sail. Photo by Mark E. Gibson

ple are on, it is apparent that they all want what is best for Orange County. "We're talking about balance," says Industrial League President Todd Nicholson, "balance between growth and adequate infrastructure and services to support that demand."

Larry Agran, Irvine's mayor, sums it up (OCR 11/23/86) by saying that "growth must be related to our ability to manage it and maintain our quality of life . . . The truth is, we have a legal and moral authority to strike a balance."

That balance will only be achieved, says Kathryn G. Thompson (president and chief executive officer of A&C Properties—SCM 10/87), "through the serious commitment and total cooperation of everyone involved, not government leaders and developers alone, but the entire citizenry as well."

What could, ultimately, be one "white knight" for easing traffic congestion and accommodating future growth is the concept of clustered environments: mini-city cores within Orange County that include substantial population, jobs, housing, business centers, cultural institutions, and entertainment.

These interdependent communities, which are springing up in metropolitan regions across the nation (for example, in Atlanta, Phoenix, St. Louis, New York, and Baltimore) already have their counterparts in Orange County. The Santa Margarita Company's new town, Rancho Santa Margarita (in South County) is one such development; and the Costa Mesa/Irvine/Newport Beach area is another, according to real estate analyst Charles Leinberger, who defines these high-density concentrations as "urban villages," saying that they offer suburban living with urban conveniences.

Leinberger (a managing partner at the Beverly Hills-based Robert Charles Lesser & Company, which specializes in urban affairs) writes (AM 10/86): "The Costa Mesa/Irvine/Newport Beach complex provides a good example of how the urban-village phenomenon is reshaping greater Los Angeles . . . [The] complex today is California's third-largest downtown, as measured by office and business-park space."

On a smaller scale, local developer Roger Torriero, the president of Griffin Realty Corporation and an associate in BGS Partners, thinks that BGS's 66-acre multi-use commercial and residential project in Santa Ana (at the intersection of Main Street and MacArthur Boulevard, across from Hutton Centre) fits Leinberger's definition of the urban village. Such developments, Torriero believes, are the county's next evolution in land-use planning.

Orange County is familiar with planned communities such as Irvine and Rancho Santa Margarita, Torriero told the *Orange County Register* (1/21/87), and BGS Partners "is taking a similar approach to this site, addressing the realities of the automobile, the aesthetic concerns, and the community needs."

Neither space nor the purpose of this chapter allows fuller discussion of Leinberger's concept of urban villages. But one point should be made: as they evolve (and like the metropolitan area that prompted their rise in the first place), urban villages will eventually face their own tug-of-war issues concerning transportation, housing, and governmental structures.

Leinberger suggests (AM 10/86) that local governments handle the inherent growth pressures by creating "strong, effective, multi-city, multi-county agencies, and perhaps even entire government structures, that correspond to the actual economic and psychological boundaries of a metropolitan area and its urban villages." His idea recalls the council of governments study undertaken by the Orange County Board of Supervisors (mentioned earlier in this chapter), to bring together elected city and county officials to coordinate issues of regional interest.

The clustering of homes, jobs, and entertainment opportunities in a single area, with easy access to adjoining "villages" containing their own specialized features, appears to offer a practical and efficient solution to growth, especially in view of Orange County's changing transportation patterns, its need to retain a solid labor base, its increasing land values, and its growing economic emphasis on technology and services ("clean" industries that, when compared to manufacturing, people are more willing to live near).

Also, eschewing the urban mainstream for the "new suburbs" is made possible and more attractive through the availability of sophisticated communications systems, which allow individuals and companies to relocate

A pool reflects the lovely Mission San Juan Capistrano. Photo by Chris Bryant

An array of exotic flowers and plants are housed at Sherman Gardens in Corona del Mar. Photo by Mark E. Gibson

and still readily conduct daily business.

Even with the potential need for greater planning to govern the organization of these self-contained communities, their presence in Orange County (either as new, master-planned towns or urban villages created within older cities) demonstrates, once again, Orange Countians' innovative thinking and their ability to be on the cutting edge concerning demands of the twenty-first century.

Orange County's leadership is constantly manifesting itself in new and encouraging ways. For example, consider the emergence of the Vietnamese Chamber of Commerce in 1981 and the Hispanic Chamber of Commerce in January 1987. Both have increasing memberships based on very productive business communities, which are supported by a strong ethnic (and a blossoming non-ethnic) consumer market.

The Hispanic Chamber of Commerce's goal, says Vice President Carole Vargas (founder and president of Carole Investments, in Santa Ana), is to network with Hispanic businesses in Orange County, and to interact with other ethnic business groups through the Orange County Minority Business Council, which includes the Hispanic and Vietnamese Chambers of Commerce, the Korean Chamber of Commerce, and the Black Business Alliance.

The Vietnamese business community (see chapters 3 and 5) "has sprung up from almost zero in the last ten years, and it makes a sizeable contribution to the local economy," says Loc T. Nguyen (the executive director of the Vietnamese Chamber of Commerce, located in Garden Grove). "The main factor [for the success of minority businesses] is that the economy has been growing and there is a good economic base, so the minorities feel less threatened economically. There is enough for everybody."

The process of Vietnamese integration into the community, Nguyen says, "has gone rather smoothly, partly because of Orange County's diversified economy, and also because we've been lucky to have leaders from both sides, American and Vietnamese, who have been aware of possible tension and worked to alleviate the problems."

As with other aspects of Orange County, any discussion of leadership is, of necessity, limited by virtue of its scope. Many other examples from among local government, business, or social leaders could have been selected to illustrate who is at the helm of California's third-largest county.

But the direction and vitality of the region derives from more than official "helmsmen." Point, if you can, to another county that has built so much in so little time. Point to another county that has become an economic powerhouse, generating interest from around the world. Based on the area's accomplishments, every Orange Countian is a leader, because everyone contributes somehow to the industrious, imaginative, and homogeneous spirit that defines Orange County.

The population is relatively young, ethnically diverse, and provides an excellent labor pool for business, and a receptive market for goods and services. The people are well educated, cultured, caring, and informed.

It is not without some validity that *Money* magazine (8/87) ranked Orange County as the tenth-best place (of 300 cities) in the U.S. to live, ahead of Los Angeles, San Francisco, and San Diego.

Certainly there is discord and controversy. But it is through the sieve of differences that ideas, opinions, and problems are sifted, separating the husks of disagreement from the seeds of compromise.

And although the county will not continue to grow at the rate of the past 30 years, it will go on growing "forever," says the whimsical author Ray Bradbury, in his introduction to *Orange County*, "or until they run out of borrowed hourglass-sand or have to jog next door to Mexico to borrow a cup of sun."

Since 1889, when it officially became the County of Orange, the county has sustained an image of continuity through time.

It is a link that often extends through generations of many families who have lived and worked here; who have tilled the soil as farmers and then put the land to other uses as economics dictated; and who have set up businesses and watched them develop and mature with the changing fortunes and opportunities of the passing decades (like First American Title Insurance Company, which was also founded in 1889, as Orange County Title Company, by C.E. Parker; and which today is among the three largest title insurance firms in the nation, headed by D.P. Kennedy, the founder's grandson).

This element of partnership emanating from people with common endeavors and interests—between those who have died, those still living, and those yet to be born—is what gives Orange County its special character; and, on the eve of its centennial, truly gives Orange Countians a reason for celebration.

Sunlight warms the Koll Center in Irvine. Photo by Yana Bridle

AFTERWORD

In *Orange County: An Economic Celebration,* Janet Graebner has vividly described where Orange County is today, and has movingly detailed the county's rapid transformation from agriculture to suburb and from suburb to urban center.

Now, as Orange County reaches its centennial, it has evolved into one of the nation's premier centers of commerce and industry, and has at the same time emerged as one of the world's most desirable settings for discretionary living.

Orange County has attained that fine but elusive formula for which the entire world searches: a seemingly unlimited economic opportunity, with a balance of employment in a range of industrial, retail, service, and technological endeavors; and at the same time has created a fabled lifestyle, with picturesque communities sheltered by a perfect climate, a seacoast location, and an ever-enriching blend of educational and cultural experiences.

The question, then, has to be asked whether these near-Utopian conditions can continue—or indeed, even blossom to an ever greater extent—as Orange County enters the twenty-first century and the decades beyond.

One certainty is that Orange County will continue to change. Perhaps, as the county matures, its changes during the next three decades will be less rapid than those during the past three, but change it will. Whether that transformation will be pleasing to current and future residents depends on the orientation of each.

As we look ahead, we see a more mature and involved county, a more cosmopolitan and urban county, and a county in a position of national and world leadership.

Not everyone who lives in Orange County today will like the Orange County of, say, the year 2010, just over two decades away. But others will believe—as they have in the past—that it is the greatest place on earth, and many envious onlookers around the world will agree.

As the county finally builds out its open land to the south, and continues to redevelop its older sections to the north, population growth will gradually decrease. Moreover, the great majority of the growth that does take place will be from Orange County births rather than from immigration, a trend already taking place. This will result in a population majority of second-, third-, and fourth-generation Orange Countians, a population more concerned and involved with their native habitat than were their ancestors, who came from Los Angeles, the Midwest, and the eastern U.S.

The natives will provide stronger leadership, and broader participation in political, civic, cultural, and social affairs, and they will show more inclination to contribute financially to local social needs and to cultural and educational institutions.

At the same time, the fabric of the population will be changing. Orange County will continue to shift from an essentially homogeneous Anglo-Christian population to a varied community of different races and religions as the Hispanic and Asian populations grow faster than

the Anglos.

But because Orange County is made up of many small-to-medium cities, each with an employment base and with residential neighborhoods, the county has every opportunity to avoid the flight of Anglos to distant sectors, as has happened in other parts of the nation. Orange County can—and shows signs that it will—become integrated, with Anglos sharing each of the cities with ethnic minorities.

Commerce and industry have established a solid base in Orange County, and that base will continue to feed upon itself synergistically and will continue to expand. The result will be the creation of far more employment opportunities, requiring more office space and support facilities; and there will be a continuing need for more employees, drawn evermore from surrounding counties.

As the need for office space grows, so will the size of the office buildings—into the air. And these will be followed by higher-rise hotels and, finally, apartment and condominium housing.

Thus, Orange County—which today boasts several "downtowns"—will itself become a countywide downtown serving the needs of its own residents as well as those of surrounding counties. They will come to Orange County for employment, for the better restaurants and shopping opportunities, for major league culture, and for active and passive recreation.

Moreover, as Orange County continues to take its place on the international scene, as a favorite for foreign investment and as an exporter of technological products, the county will become even more cosmopolitan and sophisticated.

Congestion? Urban problems? Perhaps. And perhaps not. There are urban areas of the world that suffer from the ills that accompany urban life, and there are those that do not. If Orange County is known for anything besides its weather and its location, it is admired for its fantastically innovative and highly entrepreneurial population.

There is every reason to believe, that those innovators and entrepreneurs—and their children and grandchildren—who so quickly transformed Orange County from agriculture to an urban center, can and will lead Orange County into its inevitable future as a worldwide model of "the good life."

Martin A. Brower
Editor and Publisher
Orange County Report

ABOVE: These children are getting friendly with the birds at Mission San Juan Capistrano. Photo by Mark E. Gibson

TOP LEFT: Dana Point Harbor is home base for these sailboats. Photo by Chris Bryant

TOP RIGHT: A whale waves hello off Dana Point. Photo by Chris Bryant

Office towers rise from Newport Center. Photo by Yana Bridle

ORANGE COUNTY'S ENTERPRISES

The sun slips below the horizon at the end of a peaceful day. Photo by Robert Miller

MANUFACTURING

Producing goods for individuals and industry, manufacturing firms provide employment for many Orange County area residents.

Allergan, Inc., 130-131

CalComp, Inc., 132-133

Connector Technology, Inc., 134

Fluidmaster, Inc., 135

Ford Aerospace—Aeronutronic Division, 136-137

Kimberly-Clark Corporation, 138-139

Emulex, 140-141

Ciba-Geigy Corporation, 142-143

Solmar Corporation, 144-145

Unisys Corporation, 146-147

ALLERGAN, INC.

Allergan's formula for success combines several major elements: traditional values, contemporary business practices, and advanced technology. This blend has produced the Orange County firm known as the world'sleader in eye care prescription ophthalmics, diagnostic instruments, intraocular lenses, and contact lenses and care products.

Because of its competitive mind set that encourages innovation, Allergan has created a comprehensive approach to eye care through both products and services. Research oriented, the company emphasizes its leadership position by investing 10 percent of its gross revenues in research and development annually. Some results include a specialized cataract surgery technique using an ultrasonic instrument; Ultrazyme™, a product that removes stubborn protein from contact lenses; and an analyzing device that allows doctors to see the back of the eye.

Over the past 10 years the firm has maintained an annual compound growth rate of more than 20 percent. Behind that growth is a deliberate corporate decision to concentrate on high-potential medical specialties—to know clinicians' and patients' needs, and develop a full line of products accordingly.

Allergan was established 40 years ago as a combination product/service company by Gavin Herbert, Sr. His first products were two decongestants, and his first facility was a small room over one of his pharmacies in Los Angeles. Today Allergan, Inc., with more than 6,000 employees worldwide, does business in 70-plus countries, with annual sales of more than $550 million.

In 1980 Allergan merged with health care leader SmithKline Beckman Corporation, which markets products in more than 120 countries and has approximately 34,000 employees worldwide. SKB defines its business segments as therapeutics—ethical pharmaceuticals, consumer, and animal health care products; eye and skin care—or Allergan, Inc., with Herbert Laboratories; and diagnostic/analytical—principally instruments, supplies, and laboratory testing for health care and scientific research.

Allergan's Orange County presence dates from 1962, when the company was experiencing major development. Sales reached one million dollars that year, and it employed approximately 50 people. Today employees in Irvine number some 2,000, and the firm's headquarters incorporates business offices and a manufacturing facility on 28 acres. The company also has manufacturing facilities in other U.S. locations, Brazil, Canada, France, Ireland, Italy, Mexico,

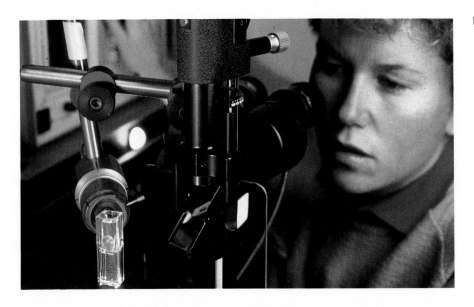

TOP: The Lens Plus® Sterile Saline Solution aerosol filling line.

LEFT: The Photon Correlator Spectrometer combines a laser, biomicroscope, and computer to analyze the protein molecules found in the lens of the eye.

Allergan, Inc., headquarters in Irvine.

Monaco, and Puerto Rico.

Under the Allergan, Inc., umbrella is a team of five health care corporate divisions, each with a special concentration, designed to meet rapid scientific advances in ophthalmic surgery and changing habits of contact lens users. The divisions operate as small businesses, but are connected by strong corporate resources.

Allergan Pharmaceuticals is a major manufacturer of prescription and over-the-counter products for treating eye disorders, including leading therapies for glaucoma, ophthalmic steroids for inflammation, ocular antibiotics, and preparations for dry eyes and allergies.

Allergan Optical is a leader in contact lenses and care products. Allergan® Enzymatic Contact Lens Cleaner, a product of the firm's own research and development, is the foremost selling contact lens product in the world, used by more than 10 million people. Other products include solutions for cleaning, disinfecting, and storing soft, hard, and gaspermeable lenses.

Allergan Medical Optics offers cataract surgeons a full line of intraocular lenses, and disposable surgical devices. Because eye surgery is a rapidly growing field and fits well within the Allergan full-service organization, AMO is expected to grow as a vital part of the corporation. It currently is one of the leading producer of intraocular lenses, which are implanted to restore cataract patients' vision.

Allergan Humphrey holds a preeminent position as pioneer of major advances in lens and cor-

neal analysis, visual field testing, and refraction. The group is a market leader in the field of computer-based diagnostic ophthalmic instruments. The company's retinal analyzer actually allows the physician to see the back of the eye, measure it digitally, and note minute changes.

Allergan International manufacturers and distributes products from the other four Allergan companies outside the United States. Global business contributes about one-third of Allergan's sales, and is expected to represent more than 40 percent in the near future.

In addition to Allergan eye care specialties, Herbert Laboratories, a part of the family but organized separately, develops and markets a full line of ethical dermatology products for the treatment of numerous skin diseases.

New eye care procedures and products are continuing to make the current headlines. A case in point is the recently developed technique for cataract surgery, called phacoemulsification. This process makes use of a small, highly sophisticated ultrasonic instrument that is introduced into the eye through a very narrow incision. Localized high-frequency sound waves break up the cataract nucleus into minute fragments, which are then gently suctioned out through the instrument's hollow tubing.

Allergaen was first to launch an ophthalmic product in the category of nonsteroidal anti-inflammatory agents in the United States. Called Ocufen™, it is an important drug used prior to cataract surgery that helps maintain es-

sential pupil dilation.

The Lens Plus® Oxysept® disinfection system for soft contact lenses has made its mark for a number of reasons. Preservative-free, it has proven to be a safe, convenient, comfortable system that offers users an uncomplicated way to maintain lenses.

Allergan is sensitive to the need for continuing education among health care practitioners and patients alike. The company provides extensive video and print materials that stress preventive eye care and detail treatment for eye disease once it has been diagnosed.

Each year Allergan participates with the University of California, Irvine, in a major ocular therapy symposium. Foremost authorities in ophthalmology are brought together to discuss modern medical and surgical therapies, as well as clinical applications and ongoing research.

Recently the firm established the Allergan Capital and Development Investment Fund to seek out and support leading-edge technologies in eye and skin care—the technologies that will yield tomorrow's products and services. According to the Allergan, Inc., vision, the fund is one of many company commitments to creating a quality environment—in its industry, for its employees, and in the communities that help its business flourish.

CALCOMP INC.

CalComp, one of Orange County's largest electronics firms, is truly a citizen of the world. The Anaheim-based company, with revenues of more than $369 million, is equally at home doing business in the United States and Canada, as well as in 44 other foreign countries.

The firm manufactures and distributes more than 100 computer graphics products throughout the world, and has gained a reputation as a leader in the computer graphics industry. CalComp holds a major position in the plotter, digitizer, graphic display, and graphics subsystem markets. The company is focusing on the graphics peripherals business as its mainstay for future growth, and plans to offer its users the broadest-possible range of computer graphics equipment in the years to come.

CalComp was founded in Orange County in 19589, during the early days of this very young industry. The firm was structured as a fully integrated hardware manufacturing and marketing company, with the responsibility to sell its own products.

"It is significant that, when so many companies are going offshore to make their products these days, CalComp still manufactures its products here," says Bill Conlin, president and the person who is credited with directing the firm's phenomenal growth. "And we market our products throughout the world as American products." Indeed, international sales now account for more than half of CalComp's revenue.

Since Conlin joined the organization in 1983, CalComp has modernized its operating procedures, initiated world-class manufacturing, and introduced new products in every division. CalComp's mission that year was to make each product perform better than the previous product at substantially lower prices. The effort paid handsomely: The following year CalComp increased its operating profit 69 percent and sales by 28 percent.

This success story repeated itself in 1985, following the introduction of even more innovative products, including the ColorMaster color thermal transfer plotter/printer. Operating figures showed an increase of 60 percent and sales, 24 percent.

CalComp conducts a prodigious amount of research and development to maintain its leading-edge position in the industry. The com-

pany creates some of the most advanced technology in its field. CalComp concentrates on the engineering side of the computer graphics market to meet the needs of major users, who sometimes market the equipment under their own names.

The firm's marketing program is as contemporary as the industry it serves, and incorporates broad sales networks worldwide that use telemarketing, telesales, direct mail, a direct end-user sales force, original equipment manufacturers (OEMs), distributors, dealers, and resellers.

It is not uncommon for CalComp's new equipment to outperform marketing expectations. For instance, the DrawingBoard digitizer—used in CAD and graphics applications—exceeded projected sales figures in its first two months on the market.

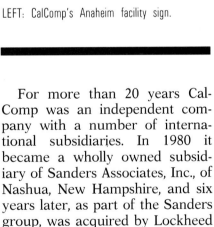

ABOVE: William Conlin, president of CalComp since 1983 and the driving force behind the company's phenomenal growth.

LEFT: CalComp's Anaheim facility sign.

For more than 20 years CalComp was an independent company with a number of international subsidiaries. In 1980 it became a wholly owned subsidiary of Sanders Associates, Inc., of Nashua, New Hampshire, and six years later, as part of the Sanders group, was acquired by Lockheed Corporation.

There are about 1,200 employees in the Orange County facility. Another 1,500 are located in several U.S. facilities or at international subsidiaries established to serve local markets.

The firm's impressive 10-building complex at 2411 West La Palma in Anaheim has more than 430,000 square feet. It houses job activities that range from assembler to computer science Ph.D.s. CalComp executives chose to locate in the county because they saw its potential for growth.

development and propulsion valve production became increasingly important business areas to the division, too.

The Shillelagh effort continued from 1958 to 1981; Chaparral was initiated in 1965 as an interim air defense system, while Sidewinder started with research in the mid-1960s. The Sidewinder, representative of the new genre of weaponry produced by the company, has been called the most effective short-range, air-to-air missile in the world. Ford Aerospace is one of the leading producers of guidance and control sections for the missile, and has manufactured more than 100,000 units. Aeronutronic extended the Shillelagh stabilization technology and created the electro-optical targeting payloads such as Pave Tack, F/A-18 FLIR, and Aquila FLIR. These payloads provide for day/night/adverse weather precision attack of fixed and moving targets by electro-optical guided weapons.

Aeronutronic has stayed in the

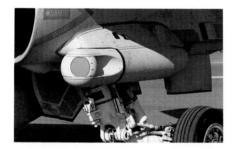

forefront of defense weapon innovation through extensive research and development activity, which has resulted in numerous technological spin-offs and product improvements. Modern facilities and state-of-the-art equipment support the firm's research efforts.

The Division is actively engaged in the development of advanced infrared detectors and charge-coupled devices (CCDs), and the study of advanced concepts in focal plane arrays and digital processing. In addition, the Division is active in passive RF technology research and development. Applications of these technologies include missile guidance, night vision, laser radar, target tracking, and weapons fire control systems.

Specific development projects include advanced seekers for a variety of missile systems applications, guided projectiles that are designed for both chemically and electromagnetically powered guns, and ceramic composite antenna windows for high-speed environments. The Division produced the antenna windows and control valves for the Trident C-4 reentry vehicle, and is working on those for the Trident D-5 and others. Radar data-processing and signature analysis are also high on the list of current projects.

Aeronutronic has won many awards and citations over the

years for product excellence and for community involvement. Company officials point to the Division's Core Values as the reason why.

Several years ago the Division adopted the well-structured, goal-oriented program to state the firm's case for quality and excellence. The main tenets apply to both personal and company performance, dedication to customer satisfaction, importance of people as individuals, and integrity—"in everything we do." The guidelines encourage hearty employee participation to meet the objectives.

Ford's involvement in Orange County philanthropy predates the Aeronutronic Division. The Ford Foundation helped support the Boy Scouts of America's Jamboree in Newport Beach in 1953, hence, the naming of Jamboree Road and Ford Road.

Aeronutronic and its employees work with a long list of local groups, including the YMCAs, Police Explorers, Boy and Girl Scouts, and cultural and educational organizations. The Corporation shares a special affinity with the Olympics, identifying with its competitive nature. Ford acquired a flagpole from the VIII Winter Olympic Games and installed it in front of the Administration Building as a symbol of the competitive spirit.

ABOVE LEFT: Ford Aerospace developed the F/A-18 FLIR infrared imaging and tracking system currently in production for installation on the U.S. Navy and Marine Corps Hornet aircraft.

LEFT: Ford Aerospace developed and manufactured the U.S. Army's Chaparral air defense system that is deployed worldwide.

KIMBERLY-CLARK CORPORATION

On 65 acres along Orangethorpe Avenue in Fullerton is a Kimberly-Clark Corporation manufacturing facility whose products carry brand names recognized throughout the United States—in some cases, the world. Names such as KLEENEX® facial tissue, HUGGIES® disposable diapers, KOTEX® and NEW FREEDOM® feminine pads, DEPEND® incontinence products, and HI-DRI® household towels.

The plant, like the City of Fullerton itself, has been a significant part of Orange County's dramatic growth. There were some 200 employees when the plant started production in 1956; today there are almost 800, and the plant injects roughly $100 million annually into the area economy in the form of payroll, locally purchased supplies and services, and taxes.

With nearly 1.2 million square feet of floor space, the Fullerton plant is so large that some maintenance employees and supervisors use vehicles to make their rounds. Manufacturing around the clock, seven days a week, enables the plant to produce facial tissue and disposable diapers for 10 western states, Alaska, and Hawaii. The plant also is a distribution center for many other Kimberly-Clark products.

The plant's two, 100-foot-long machines for manufacturing tissue can produce enough in one day to cover a four-lane highway from Los Angeles to San Francisco. The machines together can produce 160 metric tons of tissue per day. At the time the original machine was installed, it was said to be the fastest in the world, capable of forming a mile-long, 14-foot-wide ribbon of tissue in less than two minutes.

HUGGIES® disposable diapers are turned out by 200-foot-long machines that position the diaper's many components in their proper places at precisely the right moment in a high-speed, continuous process controlled and monitored by computers and highly skilled operators.

Much of this technologically advanced, proprietary equipment was developed by Kimberly-Clark's engineering and research staff. Their expertise made possible a series of product innovations that helped make HUGGIES® diapers one of the biggest marketing success stories of all time. The Fullerton plant is one of seven Kimberly-Clark facilities that manufactures diapers in the United States.

Kimberly-Clark was founded in Neenah, Wisconsin, in 1872; its first product was newsprint made from linen and cotton rags. The firm evolved from a small newsprint maker into a large paper and forest products company, and then into today's highly diversified international corporation especially known for its consumer products. Fullerton was the site of the company's first production facility west of the Mississippi River.

In the 1950s Kimberly-Clark began looking at Pacific Coast locations for additional manufacturing facilities to avoid rising freight costs and improve service to customers. Fullerton's proximity to the large consumer market of Los Angeles was highly desirable.

Clean lines and attractively landscaped grounds of Kimberly-Clark's Fullerton plant understate its behemoth proportions. The plant has more than 27 acres of floor space. Photo courtesy of Larry C. Crosby

However, because of the area's semiarid climate, and because paper-manufacturing operations traditionally were large water users, Kimberly-Clark would have to devise exceptional water conservation practices—more extensive than any paper manufacturing plant of the time. The firm's engineers, manufacturing experts, and others accepted the challenge. The result: The new plant had the distinction of being the world's first paper-manufacturing facility to recover all of its effluent waters and to treat them for reuse in the papermaking process. Over the years the plant has maintained and improved its water conservation and treatment measures to the point that the plant today uses less water than it did in prior years, although production has been substantially increased.

While the consumer products manufactured and distributed from Fullerton are the most visible part of Kimberly-Clark, there is much more to the firm, whose annual sales rank it among the top 100 manufacturing companies in the country. When doctors enter the operating room, they may be wearing one of the firm's disposable gowns, and surgical instruments may be delivered to them in sterile wrap also produced by Kimberly-Clark. The operating room attendants may be wearing Kimberly-Clark gowns that help prevent the spread of infection. Beds in the hospital may be fitted with comfortable cushioning pads produced by a Kimberly-Clark subsidiary—pads made of movable, hollow fibers that prevent pressure points from forming and causing bedsores.

At Fullerton, Kimberly-Clark produces KLEENEX® (far right) facial tissue (Photo courtesy of Larry C. Crosby) and HUGGIES® (right) disposable diapers 24 hours a day, seven days a week.

Your newspaper may be printed on Kimberly-Clark newsprint. The letterheads of many of America's leading companies are enhanced by the fine stationery and envelopes made by Kimberly-Clark. The firm also manufactures some of the thinnest papers in the world, so the family Bible or dictionary may be printed on its paper. Many paperback books are printed on paper from Kimberly-Clark.

The organization also employs special technologies to make adhesive-coated papers, tapes, labels, and tobacco-related products such as cigarette papers, and produces base papers for other manufacturers who, in turn, convert the base papers into products such as abrasives, strippable wallpaper, and book covers.

In California, Kimberly-Clark's Karolton Envelope has manufacturing and distribution facilities at West Sacramento. In total, Kimberly-Clark has manufacturing operations in 18 states and 19 foreign countries, and its products are sold in 150 countries. It employs more than 36,000 people worldwide.

Kimberly-Clark's success has roots in business principles established by the company's founders, who agreed to manufacture the best-possible product, serve customers well, deal fairly to gain their confidence and goodwill, and deal fairly with employees. These fundamental values have guided the firm ever since. Today, as in the early days, Kimberly-Clark employees at Fullerton and around the world make the company grow by helping fill human needs and trying to build something better for tomorrow.

Kimberly-Clark Corporation's world headquarters is in suburban Dallas. The company's many business units are managed from operations headquarters in Neenah, Wisconsin, and Roswell, Georgia, near Atlanta.

® Registered Trademark of Kimberly-Clark Corporation

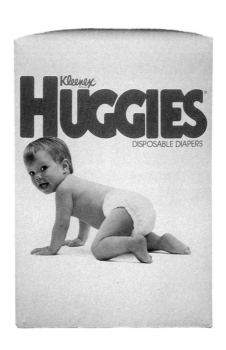

EMULEX

Emulex, a high-tech computer products company headquartered in Orange County, is the world's largest supplier of products compatible with computers from Digital Equipment Corporation, the industry's leading minicomputer maker. The Costa Mesa firm specializes in high-performance data-storage and data-communications components and systems, which it provides not only for DEC computers, but also for personal computers from IBM, and for other mini- and microcomputer systems.

Not yet 10 years old, Emulex employs 850 people (650 in Orange County) and produces revenues in excesss of $100 million per year. Its facilities on Harbor Boulevard encompass more than 200,000 square feet, much of which is dedicated to engineering and manufacturing its high-tech hardware. The company's second manufacturing plant is located in Dorado, Puerto Rico.

The firm's products range from proprietary integrated circuit chips and printed circuit board-size controllers for computer peripherals to complete data-storage subsystems priced at more than $150,000. However different in scale, all have been specifically designed for applications where additional performance is worth a premium, a strategy that continues to fuel the firm's growth.

"We are not now and have never been in the commodities business," says Fred B. Cox, chairman, chief executive officer, and founder. "Our original strategy was to make the best, highest performing products available for DEC computers, and to that end we developed an engineering strength that may be unequaled in a company of our size, plus the manufacturing expertise and worldwide sales channels necessary to make use of that strength.

"Now we are in a position to 'lev-

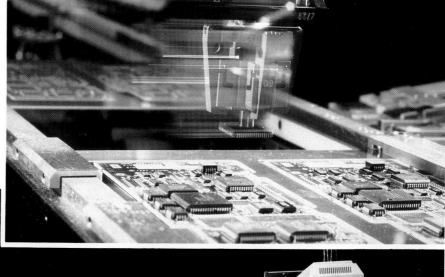

RIGHT: Emulex' total manufacturing capacity is well over 500,000 board-level products per year.

.BELOW: The company's data-storage and data-communications products are all engineered at the Costa Mesa facility, although manufacturing is done at more than one location.

erage' that proven technology to enter select marketplaces where our special skills make a difference—by extending the performance of other popular computers in the same manner we have for DEC and IBM systems."

Those marketplaces lead from Orange County all over the country and all over the world. Emulex' computer user and OEM customers are supported by the local engineering and technical staff, through regional sales/support offices throughout the United States, and through branches in Canada, the United Kingdom, Germany, France, and Australia.

Product service is provided through all of those offices and more. In the United States, for example, service is also provided through several major service firms—a list that ironically now includes DEC itself—in more than 50 metropolitan areas.

The reach of the service organization underscores what Cox calls "our absolute commitment to always meet our customers' needs." This loyalty to its customers is reflected in customer loyalty to Emulex, and the firm is proud

to list a large number of *Fortune* 500 companies among both end users and OEM purchasers of its products.

Cox emphasizes "people orientation" in house as well: "We try to create a workplace that is pleasant. We share profits. We try to have fun in what we do. And we socialize as much as possible to maintain our corporate culture."

Drivers on Harbor Boulevard may have wondered what they were witnessing from time to time as Emulex' expansive staff has streamed out into the parking lot around the buildings for "all-hands" meetings—for employee

awards, handing out profit-sharing checks, and similar activities.

Those passers by can stop wondering what Emulex' employees are up to: They're busy maintaining a unique company culture, one that seems to fit in Orange County better than it could anywhere else.

RIGHT: Products range in size from integrated circuit chips and printed circuit board-size controllers for computer peripherals to data-storage subsystems like the one above.

BELOW: The firm has invested more than $30 million in research and development—including such elements as computer-aided design and layout systems—over the past three years.

CIBA-GEIGY CORPORATION

Aircraft primary and secondary structures as well as interior cabin components aren't what they used to be. Now the parts are being created from technologically advanced composite materials—tough, lightweight, high-performance materials with properties that allow aircraft to do things they have never done before.

Ciba-Geigy Corporation, with a major facility in Anaheim, is at the forefront of the relatively new composite-manufacturing business. The industry, still in its infancy, has been compared to the electronics business of the late 1960s. It has been fueled by rapid growth in aerospace as well as by increasing materials applications found through imaginative research and development.

"The uses are nothing short of revolutionary," says Robert Siegmund, vice-president and general manager of Ciba-Geigy's Composite Materials Department (CMD) in Orange County. "Many people feel that composites offer one major advantage to aircraft manufacturers—the ability to reduce weight and conserve fuel. But composites offer many performance benefits as well. Some of the new designs could never have been accomplished with metal."

Ciba-Geigy is a leading producer of advanced composite materials, specializing in unidirectional and woven fabrics, prepregs (materials preimpregnated with resins), and adhesives, as well as honeycomb core, structural panels, and fabricated parts for the aerospace, automotive, marine shelter, and recreation industries. The company manufactures products that literally replace metal with structural composites. The lighter-weight materials have the equivalent strength of metals, allowing aircraft greater efficiency.

In North America Ciba-Geigy, with $3 billion in sales, has numerous facilities. The Anaheim unit, known as CMD (Composite Materials Department), is responsible for the corporation's U.S. composite activities. CMD is implementing a major local consolidation, culminating in 1988, that will combine 10 manufacturing, sales, and service operations at the Anaheim address.

The firm's presence in Orange County has been strong, according to management, because of Southern California's strength in both commercial and military aerospace. Ciba-Geigy, as one of the largest composite-manufacturing companies in the industry, was drawn to the region also because of its emphasis on research and development.

Locally, CMD has approximately 400 employees in a largely self-contained operation that in-

The new Anaheim headquarters of Ciba-Geigy Corporation's composite materials department.

cludes in-house research and development, project engineering, manufacturing, marketing, sales, and service. There are 150 people in Miami, which is primarily a manufacturing facility for nonmetallic honeycomb core.

The firm has deep local roots with commitment to Orange County, having grown in the area from an acquisition of Reliable Manufacturing in the mid-1970s. CMD has primary marketing responsibility for North and South America, yet it is structured to interface liberally with its international counterparts in Europe and Asia.

Ciba-Geigy Limited, the parent organization, is a publicly owned Swiss company with headquarters in Basel. It is one of the world's leading chemical-manufacturing groups, with member companies that produce a broad spectrum of products from pharmaceuticals to structural plastics.

With approximately $10 billion in sales worldwide, the firm is more than 200 years old. Its Swiss founder, Johann Rudolph Geigy, specialized in trading dyestuffs and drugs of various kinds. CIBA (an acronym for the chemical industry) was founded by Alexander Clavel as a dye house to manufacture synthetic dyes for silk. Currently it maintains major research and development, production, and sales units in some 50 countries. It has a work force of more than 80,000 worldwide.

In advanced composite materials Ciba-Geigy concentrates its operations in Western Europe and Asia as well as North America to serve the major international aerospace industry centers.

Ciba-Geigy exhibits cohesiveness among its composites group units: It pools technological resources in resin formulation and fabric engineering in order to satisfy the growing demands of the aerospace industry in the coming decade.

An employee of Ciba-Geigy Corporation manufactures graphite prepegs to be used in aerospace applications. Courtesy, Ken Whitmore, 1986

Through use of sophisticated manufacturing equipment and the latest on-stream techniques, CMD's Siegmund says the company keeps a firm grip on streamlined production capacity and effective quality control. In the new Anaheim facility, for instance, Ciba-Geigy has installed state-of-the-art equipment and laboratories worth some $50 million.

Product lines can be individual elements or finished components. The company is also structured to tailor-make products to customers' specifications. A few major examples:

Prepreg, fiber-reinforced plastics, are low in weight, high in strength, with a high level of toughness, and both fatigue and environmentally resistant. The product is used in high-performance aircraft and other transportation and industrial applications.

Adhesives, modified epoxy film, are a versatile bonding material for metals and composites. Generally high-temperature resistant and high performance, the material is used in the manufacture of large complex parts.

Honeycomb Core, used as a basic structural material, is lightweight, durable, and noncorrosive. It is used in aircraft, missile, space-vehicle, and marine applications. The material is so light and rigid that it is used in creating beams, floorboards, flaps, and tail assemblies of commercial and military aircraft. Newer uses include road and marine vehicles, sporting goods, electronics, and construction.

Woven goods from all types of synthetic and mineral fibers are woven in-house in Anaheim. The company's variety of styles offers great versatility and includes twill, unidirectional, bias, hybrid, acoustic, and custom. Ciba-Geigy fabrics have set industry standards, using space-age fibers and specialty engineering to provide design solutions for tomorrow's aircraft.

The international company, as a fast-growing, market-driven organization, prides itself on current research and development accomplishments and has set future sights on helping to forge new directions in aviation.

SOLMAR CORPORATION

You can do a lot of things with bugs these days—biologically cultivated bugs, that is, carefully formulated through laboratory processes to help solve modern society's growing environmental problems.

The bugs, or bacteria, are the mainstay of "bioaugmentation," a word coined by Solmar Corporation's president, R.B. "Jones" Grubbs. It explains his company's natural technique used for treating organic waste. "The process is centuries old in nature," Grubbs explains. "But it has become sophisticated as a biotechnology industry only during the past 10 years."

Need for the technique and its formulated products has grown as public awareness of the environment increases, and as federal and state legislators strengthen and enforce new protective laws, Grubbs points out.

Solmar Corporation, headquartered in Orange, researches, manufactures, and distributes made-to-order bacteria to treat wastewater and hazardous wastes, primarily for organic reduction and odor control. The company also operates as a consultant to evaluate ongoing problems for its clients and recommend the proper treatment.

In the laboratory, Solmar works to combat tough new wastes as well as familiar old enemies, such as sludge. The firm's product, sold under the trademark Advanced Bio Cultures, is a variety of formulations that derives from naturally occurring soil bacteria and digests only nonliving organic matter. The formulations have no additives themselves to adversely affect the environment, humans, plants, or wildlife.

Solmar's bacterial formulations must be carefully selected and matched to each project to provide the desired organic breakdowns, because no single bacteria type can deal with all wastes. There are numerous, complex interrelationships among a multitude of organisms necessary to handle the cleanup.

How is the product assembled? Individual organisms are grown in pure form, then preserved, formulated, and packaged with elaborate precautions to preclude the introduction of unwanted contaminants.

They are especially suited to degrade complex organics such as oils, greases, hydrocarbons, pesticides, and tars. Basically Solmar's formulations reduce these contaminants to harmless end products such as carbon dioxide and water.

Why use formulated bugs instead of native bacteria? In the ap-

The large Orange Sanitation Districts of Orange County plants have found the Solmar products indispensible in controlling odors.

plication to typical sewers and wastewater systems, for instance, the laboratory bacteria are more effective in breaking down some of the troublesome organics. They also can work with or without air, and they cannot produce hydrogen sulfide—which creates all kinds of problems: odors, corrosion, and toxicity, to name a few.

Solmar, under Grubbs' leadership, has contributed widely to the literature of its young industry. The company's formulations and treatment techniques have set many standards for the waste-control industry. Its eight basic formulas offer flexibility for different applications.

Solmar's physical plant, with laboratory, manufacturing, and distribution facilities, is located at 625 West Katella in Orange. It serves clients worldwide through a network of representatives.

Grubbs says Orange County is one of the best locations his type of business could have, for several reasons. The area's biotechnology emphasis offers solid support for Solmar; county and state officials have a high level of environmental awareness; and the distribution system by both truck and air helps get the product out quickly.

Solmar, founded in 1980, was acquired by Grubbs in 1984. The firm serves four primary types of clientele: industrial facilities, municipalities, hazardous waste sites, and institutional/commercial establishments such as restaurants. Many *Fortune* 500 companies use Solmar's formulations. Products have proven successful in a variety of industries as well: sewage treatment, paper, wood preservation, canning, soft-drink bottling, meat packing, dairy processing, petroleum, and petrochemical.

The restaurant business is a primary example of how Solmar's bacteria works. For instance, most establishments have grease traps on dishwashers that need to be pumped out once a month.

Through the use of bacteria cultures, that process can be eliminated, an increasingly important fact because dump sites that once accepted the material are being closed.

It is desirable to biodegrade the grease from cooking oils and food particles to save kitchen pipes and other equipment from blockages and backups. By adding these bacterial formulations to the restaurant scene, the microorganisms literally form colonies on the walls of the pipes, and biodegrade—or break up—the grease as it flows through.

There are other benefits: extending life expectancy of costly treatment facilities, eliminating costs and headaches associated with regulatory noncompliance, and reducing energy requirements for business operators. Solmar also treats another very different kind of environmental problem—decorative ponds and recreational lakes that can have odors, algae growth, and murky waters.

What do the bugs look like? The culture formulations are supplied in dry form, and become fully activated when they are presoaked in water or wastewater. They are shipped in 25-pound plastic pails for safe, protective storage.

Among Solmar Corporation's objectives, according to Grubbs, is the desire to create innovative technology that will eliminate health and environmental risks, and to simplify treatments for overburdened systems such as municipal sewerage plants. Grubbs notes: "We may not be in the business to make money for a client, but we sure do save him money."

The preserved cultures are reactivated in the field prior to being used.

UNISYS CORPORATION

Unisys Corporation is one of the world's leading manufacturers of commercial information systems, defense systems, and related services. Created from the merger of Burroughs and Sperry Corporations in 1986, Unisys has revenues of $10 billion, more than 90,000 employees, and 60,000 customers in more than 100 countries. Engineering, research, and development funding in 1987 was $1.4 billion.

The corporation has 62 major research, engineering, and manufacturing operations worldwide. Among them are facilities in Rancho Santa Margarita, Mission Viejo, and Lake Forest. Together the three locations form Product and Technology Operations. More than 2,000 employees design, manufacture, and market mainframe computer and computer components. Unisys Orange County is also involved in software design and development.

Approximately 350 Unisys employees work in the state-of-the-art manufacturing facility in Rancho Santa Margarita. The 115,000-square-foot complex is located on six acres of a new master-planned community.

Major products manufactured there are the Unisys A Series and V Series mainframe computer systems. These technologically advanced entry and medium-range systems are designed to handle a wide variety of data-processing applications. Card assembly for these systems are manufactured in Rancho Santa Margarita as well.

Additional design and manufacture of the A and V Series computers are performed at the 3,302-square-foot facility in Mission Viejo, just six miles from Rancho Santa Margarita.

In Lake Forest, approximately 340 employees are engaged in developing software for the A Series and V Series systems.

While Unisys software and hardware represent some of the most advanced capabilities in the industry, the company's approach remains highly personal. "This is fundamentally a people-oriented business," says David F. DeVinny, vice-president and plant general manager of the Systems Manufacturing Group. "While we know our success and growth are dependent on many factors, we place great stock in the skills, intelligence, and dedication of our employees."

Paramount to Unisys' people-oriented approach to business is career development for employees. The corporation conducts extensive in-house management and professional training courses and encourages employees to attend workshops, seminars, and classes customized to the local area and disciplines.

"We established an achievement plan to recognize and reward innovative thinking and individual initiative on specific projects or assignments that help the company meet its goals," says Michael J. Irving, vice-president, Systems Engineering Entry/Medium A Series. "Employees can earn awards up to $100,000 for suggestions that the corporation implements."

This attention to employees benefits Unisys products.

"Our rich, fully featured operating system is second to none in the industry," says Sam Samman, vice-president of A Series Software. "It provides the basis upon which the most flexible and efficient transaction-processing capabilities can be efficiently developed using third- or fourth-generation languages."

The A1, smallest member of the A Series family of Unisys computer systems. Photo by Gary Million

BUSINESS AND PROFESSIONS

Greater Orange County's professional community brings a wealth of service, ability, and insight to the area.

Orange County Chamber of Commerce, 150

Deloitte Haskins & Sells, 151

First American Title Insurance Company, 152-153

Gateway Computer, 154-156

PCM (Professional Community Management), 157

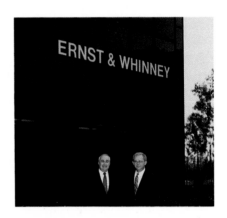

Ernst & Whinney, 158-159

Hutton Center is among the many new office buildings that grace Costa Mesa. Photo by Yana Bridle

Fred. S. James & Co. of California, Inc., 160

ORANGE COUNTY CHAMBER OF COMMERCE

Orange County's traditional historic image as a rural community—until the past couple of decades—may not be quite correct.

"Agrarian, yes. Rural in the true sense of the word, no," says Lucien D. Truhill, president and chief executive officer of the Orange County Chamber of Commerce. "The county was an agricultural empire, with landed aristocracy who often sent their children to Harvard, Yale, Bryn Mawr, and Vassar. They marketed their Valencia oranges 'Back East,' while importing a lot of established eastern practices to the county—such as well-structured government, an excellent road system, and superb educational institutions."

This legacy helped shape the Orange County Chamber of Commerce, which for more than 75 years has played a distinctive role in developing the economic health of the community. Today the chamber, with its 1,700 member companies, is the primary unifying business group in a sophisticated urban metroplex with 27 cities and a large unincorporated area. No one city or section of the county is dominant.

Headquartered in central Orange County in the City of Orange, the chamber gives its members access to the county's business and industrial base through a variety of avenues. They include a comprehensive business and industrial directory of 5,600 company names, vital statistics, and key personnel; "Golden 500"—Orange County's 500 largest employing units; newspapers/newsletters with business information; active councils that address pressing county issues that have a major impact on business such as transportation, economic planning, governmental affairs, energy, and environment; and executive luncheons and breakfasts that feature influential speakers who discuss topics of importance to the

Lucien D. Truhill, president and chief executive officer of the Orange County Chamber of Commerce.

business community.

"Our councils have been particularly influential reviewing and recommending legislation, and working closely with the county's many administrative agencies as well as networking with organizations both in the public and private sectors," Truhill notes.

The recent influx of foreign business with specialized chambers of commerce has not altered the Orange County chamber's role. If anything, the constantly diversifying economy has focused an ever greater need for its leadership. In fact, the Orange County Chamber of Commerce—noted for its strength, stability, and unity of purpose—has been at the forefront in emphasizing the need for Pacific Rim interaction. It helped assist in founding two influential world trade and marketing groups in the county—Orange County Chapter, World Trade Center Association, and the O.C. International Marketing Association.

Upcoming challenges for the Orange County Chamber of Commerce include establishment of a Small Business Development Center, as well as developing new programs in the area of transportation and water and waste management as needed to ensure the chamber's leadership as the voice of business and industry for Orange County.

Ninety percent of the chamber's membership is involved in small business, reflecting Orange County's well-publicized entrepreneurial reputation. Truhill states this preponderance of successful self-starters fosters a special business spirit and dynamism. "Such character has made us an economic star in the crown of the American free enterprise system," he says. It might be noted that it is a crown that Orange County continues to wear with ease.

DELOITTE HASKINS & SELLS

More than 20 years ago Deloitte Haskins & Sells made a dual commitment to Orange County: to help businesses build a major commercial center there, and to work toward quality growth in the area through community involvement.

Since then DH&S, as a prominent public accounting, tax, and consulting firm, has realized phenomenal growth of its own. What was once a small office in Santa Ana with four employees has become a major professional services group of more than 200 persons located in Costa Mesa at 695 Town Center Drive.

As part of the international DH&S firm, now the sixth-largest accounting firm in worldwide revenues, the local office joins a network of more than 400 units in 79 countries. In the United States, Deloitte Haskins & Sells is one of the fastest-growing accounting and consulting firms. "We see Orange County's profile continuing to rise, not only in California but nationally and internationally," says C. Stephen Mansfield, partner in charge. "Although our firm spans the globe in providing a myriad of specialized services, each practice office focuses on local needs and issues, and develops specific industry expertise."

Mansfield notes that being deeply rooted as a local entity, DH&S shares in the county's prosperity and returns the favor as a matter of policy. To that end, DH&S serves close to 100 nonprofit groups and charities through both individual and corporate contributions and volunteer time, says Mansfield. The groups that benefit include health care, the arts, education, and civic, youth, and professional associations.

DH&S serves a broad-based clientele in Orange County's diverse economy: real estate, high technology, financial services, health care, retail food service, government agencies, and other indus-

ABOVE: Volunteers from Deloitte Haskins & Sells at the Annual United Way Sand Castle Contest in Seal Beach. Their two-headed dragon took first place in the Professional Leadership Division of this kick-off fund-raising campaign.

RIGHT: Members of the Deloitte Haskins & Sells management team reviewing a document on site, at the client's printing facility.

tries. The firm works with large institutions as well as start-up companies in providing audit, tax planning, management advisory, strategic planning, and productivity services.

In recent years DH&S has developed a wide range of specialty services and products using advanced technology to help clients meet today's fast-paced business environment. Company experts have reshaped the basic nature of auditing through the use of microcomputers, and have developed a number of application programs for staff and client use. Most noteworthy among them are PlusPlan, a financial modeling, consolidation, and reporting system; STAR, Statistical Techniques for Analytical Review; ControlPlan; and Estimation Sampling.

New programs are continually under development, as are computer seminars to help familiarize clients with innovative information systems. A forward-thinking Emerging Business Services group helps clients gain a broad business perspective in finance, administration, and purchasing, and the Capital Connection network for entrepreneurs identifies the best-possible financing alternatives.

Management points to several reasons for the company's outstanding growth: Deloitte Haskins & Sells uses a comprehensive quality-control system to maintain high professional standards, and makes a significant investment in recruiting new talent—in keeping with the vitality of Orange County's image.

FIRST AMERICAN TITLE INSURANCE COMPANY

tered in Santa Ana, just three blocks from its original office, which opened in 1889. The company has grown from two to more than 6,000 employees. It was established only 13 years after the practice of title insurance was begun in the United States.

It was a colorful era, with land at the center of the Old West's appeal. Settlers flocked to the frontier to take advantage of land grants, government auctions, pri-

When Donald Parker Kennedy, then executive vice-president of the company, took his expansion plan to the board of directors, he was given a succinct response: "We're not interested—but if you want to, we'll go along." Today Kennedy, as president and chief executive officer of The First American Financial Corporation of Santa Ana and its principal subsidiary, First American Title Insurance Company, oversees one of the largest (and oldest) title insurers in the country—with assets of more than $297 million.

First American has a sizable national presence, thanks to Kennedy's growth strategy of acquiring established companies in major markets, creating new ones, soliciting business from independent brokers, and converting abstract firms. Today First American, approaching its 100th year in business, is represented in all the large national markets, operating through a network of more than 2,500 branch offices, subsidiaries, affiliates, or agents in all 50 states. First American also provides title services abroad—in Guam, Mexico, Puerto Rico, the Virgin Islands, and England.

Two specific additions strengthened First American's national network in recent years: Columbia Real Estate Title Insurance Com-

pany on the East Coast, which does some 17.5 percent of the title business in the District of Columbia, and Security Title Corporation in Hawaii, which as a new agent doubled the firm's policy coverage in the state.

The premise for title insurance is simple, but the process is complex: It protects ownership of real property against the many possibilities of loss due to title defects, liens, and encumbrances. In a real estate sale, it is the title insurance company's task to make sure the seller is reflecting the title of the land accurately. Specialists search records, maps, and other documents affecting the land parcel in question to protect potential buyers and lenders who make loans secured by real property.

First American is headquar-

TOP LEFT: First American Title Insurance Company's national headquarters in Santa Ana.

ABOVE: The Title Department—heart of the firm's business.

vate land sales, and many other so-called opportunities that all too often proved to be fraudulent. Then, as now, there was a need for an orderly method of transferring land titles and protecting property ownership.

First American's predecessor, Orange County Title Company, grew out of two abstract firms operating in Santa Ana when Orange County itself became a legal entity in 1889. Company founder Charles E. Parker successfully consolidated the two by 1894, and set out to build a conservatively run, financially sound service organization.

In its nearly 100 years of business there have been few changes in top management, with only four company presidents, three of which have been members of the founding family. Founder C.E. Parker was followed by H.A. Gardener, who was succeeded by C.E.'s son, George A. Parker, who in turn was succeeded by his nephew and grandson of the founder, current president and chief executive officer Donald P. Kennedy. Four generations have served First American's management, with Parker S. Kennedy, the founder's great-grandson, currently serving as executive vice-president.

The family tradition extends beyond business to notable community service and loyalty to the home base in which the organization thrives. Long employee tenure is commonplace, with service dates of 35 years and longer proving the family atmosphere.

If the company culture has remained constant over the decades, its industry has shown marked changes. For one thing, today's

business environment, influenced by tax reform and greater availability of real estate investment funds, has led to a number of record-breaking years in earnings for First American. Still conservatively run and financially sound, the firm's phenomenal growth nationwide has occurred primarily within the past three decades under the expansion plan that Kennedy proposed in 1958. He is credited with building the international organization through a well-managed program and cultivated teamwork.

Kennedy's management philosophy is to encourage regional autonomy and avoid corporate red tape that seems inherent in large corporate structures. Yet he insists on strict accounting controls to maintain management involvement in the geographically diverse system. And he encourages maintaining a personal touch throughout, in keeping with the founder's style.

One way to do so is to offer services that are responsive to clients' special needs. For example, First American provides national title service for major corporations with real estate ventures that cross state or regional lines. This one-source assistance in all title matters, from planning to final closing, simplifies what could be a highly complicated procedure.

While title insurance is First

President and chief executive officer Donald P. Kennedy.

American's primary business, its trust subsidiary contributes heartily to revenues by managing personal and employee benefit trust accounts, as well as assets for private, custodian, and agency accounts, with fiduciary assets in excess of $.25 billion.

While the founding family still directs operations, the firm is no longer family held. First American stock was first traded publicly in 1964. Today its stock is listed on the NASDAQ National Market System.

The management of First American Title Insurance Company prides itself on blending forward-thinking business techniques with past-proven values as the firm approaches its centennial celebration.

LEFT: Prior to issuance of a title insurance policy, a search is conducted into the history of a piece of property. Lot books contain records from the beginning of the county in 1889, to 1965, when a geographic plant was set up.

RIGHT: Beginning in 1965 documents pertaining to property were placed in folders for ready access by title searchers. This geographic plant holds all documents recorded until 1983, when the title plant went on computer.

GATEWAY COMPUTER

Gateway Computer, a full-service company that provides computer technologies for its customers, operates under a simple job description: Gateway Computer personnel are Partners in Business Solutions with their customers in a work environment that is often cluttered with confusing computer- and technology-related issues.

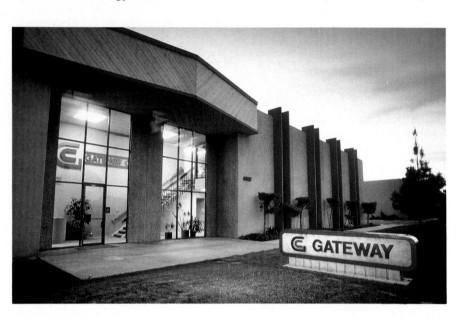

Gateway's role is that of a catalyst, moving companies toward growth through the right computer solutions. As a product reseller with extensive technical systems support, training, and service capabilities, Gateway specializes in working with corporate customers. The firm has established strategic relationships with leading industry manufacturers, whose products best serve business solutions and whose continuing research and development yield the latest in technology.

Gateway Computer, headquartered in Huntington Beach, has some 180 employees throughout its 10-branch system. Its field business centers average about 18 employees per office. All product shipping emanates from the corporate headquarters, with each branch responsible for all other regional needs. Gateway has offices in all

metropolitan areas of California, with one in Las Vegas and one in Chicago.

The company was established as a reseller in 1979, about the same time the microcomputer was introduced. As Gateway Computer System, it sold a wide range of products and services, including personal computers, and experi-

Gateway Computer's corporate headquarters in Huntington Beach.

enced a number of rapid growth years from 1981 to 1984, including being on *Inc.* magazine's list of fastest growing companies in America in 1985.

In 1987, under new management and with a new team approach, Gateway continued to strengthen its position with the *Fortune* 1,000 customer. Gateway's customers typically are large corporations or utilities, with a mix of industries such as aerospace, financial services, insurance, accounting, law, and varied manufacturing. There are no cash registers in Gateway's branch offices, no supplies of diskettes for the casual customer to buy. Rather

the offices are centers for advance computer solicitors.

"In an innovation-driven business, it is easy to lose sight of our real purpose—providing the best-possible service and support for our customers," says Rick Selvage, chief executive officer. Selvage, who has been called the quintessential One-Minute Manager, continues: "Our role is to use creative thinking toward new and better ways to get the job done, to make a wide variety of resources available to the customers, including the right product and the best business solutions in application, in a cost-effective way for our customer."

Selvage is representative of the new management team, using an energetic, dedicated, high-profile approach. He frequently visits customers on site to stay in touch with customers' needs and to demonstrate the availability of all Gateway's management.

"Dynamic" has become the marketing byword, notes Michael Ross, director of marketing. "We have a young, vital company with an ambitious staff that is committed to solving customers' needs. Our charter is to be innovative not in product, which we leave up to the manufacturers, but in application and service."

Gateway's relatively small staff is structured to be flexible and responsive to new ideas and products in the marketplace, and make them immediately available to customers. While the company uses many manufacturers, IBM is the product most suited to Gateway's corporate customer. Says Ross, "Their systems integration capabilities are quite extensive, and their attention to specific kinds of business gives us great latitude in applications." Other prominent products in the Gateway repertoire include Compaq, Hewlett-Packard, Intel, and Apple Computer.

Gateway, as a reseller, shares in the technology-oriented decision making for the customer with the product manufacturer acting as a conduit. To satisfy this need, Gateway has taken great care to align itself with some of the most resourceful suppliers in the industry. The firm's own systems engineers and system consultants develop customized solutions for customers' needs, such as networking, micro-to-mainframe communications, advanced systems, multi-user systems, internetwork communications, and many others.

Technical support, headed by Martin Schwarz, director of technologies, is an important part of the Gateway structure. With systems engineers operating from headquarters and through the local centers, the advanced systems group offers two levels of support to customers: backup on highly specialized systems, and integrated service on software and hardware by working closely with Gateway's hardware specialists, the Service Group.

"The name of the game is customer satisfaction," says Tom Halloran, general services manager. "Once you've established a system to make that happen, it's easy to maintain." Halloran's approach is straightforward: "Give the customers what they want—plus 10 percent more—and charge a fair

The Gateway Special Applications Group combines technical knowledge with industry-specific experience to create solutions that better meet customers' needs.

price."

Nearly 50 technicians comprise the service department in the field and at the corporate headquarters. They work through a central dispatching system, and use a highly efficient method for stocking the most up-to-date parts companywide.

Technicians work closely with vendors to receive in-factory

BELOW LEFT: Each business center has complete training facilities using the most up-to-date equipment.

BELOW RIGHT: Fully equipped and operational demonstration areas are the focal point of Gateway Business Centers.

training for warranty and maintenance work, as well as familiarity training on new products as soon as they are announced. Gateway's policy is to train all its technicians for proficiency on all systems, not just as specialists who can handle only one line.

"This gives our staff greater depth and a competency level that sets them apart," notes Halloran. "The qualities I look for when I'm hiring these specialists are about 80 percent personality—the ability to interface with people—10 percent technical ability, and 10 percent logistics skills in conducting the operations. The latter two can be taught, but you can't instill an interest in serving people."

Training is an integral part of the new Gateway, however, according to Lorraine Watkins, training services manager in charge of both consumer and in-house programs. Corporate forums on new products are an important part of the training services for clients, taught on site or at Gateway facil-

ities. There are also regular classes on basic programs such as Lotus, and there are application-specific courses.

One of the most popular is in the growing field of desk-top publishing. Gateway's course on newsletter layouts, an introduction to concepts, is hands-on training. Participants are encouraged to bring actual work into the seminar so they can walk out with a finished product. Another avant garde yet useful course is on business presentations—sophisticated graphics for print, overhead transparencies, interactive video on disks, and so on.

"Our company is introducing more leading-edge tactics all the time," says Watkins, explaining the high-end training that is becoming Gateway's specialty. A new feature, the Gateway Class Pass, allows the holder to attend virtually every course offered for one year, with programs available to systems customers and the general public alike.

The Gateway Special Applications Group addresses a growing concern among corporate customers. "Our customer's needs have evolved past the point of simple supply and maintenance of equip-

ment," says Selvage. "The key now is to be able to provide full featured, integrated systems for specific applications such as Computer Aided Design, Medical or Legal Office Management, or Accounting," Our Special Applications division has hired people with technical knowledge and specific industry experience to better solve these needs.

An exciting addition to Gateway's divisional structure is the Gateway Direct division. Gateway Direct oversees both catalog sales and Bid Desk operations. The Gateway Computer Buyer's Guide has close to 1,000 selected items accompanied by compatibility matrices to facilitate selection and features immediate delivery. The Bid Desk offers special pricing for orders meeting minimum quantity criteria.

Attention to detail is a common thread throughout the Gateway organization, explains Jeff Sweet, telemarketing and customer service manager. "We follow up on every single customer order to get feedback. Once we capture the data, we can offer support to our sales force, service personnel, and senior management."

Sweet believes this meticulous

consultation with customers, a priority with Gateway's management, has done much to build the Partners in Business Solutions capability. Says Sweet, "We make personal contact by telephone. We don't rely on a written survey. We ask specific questions with a rating system that in effect is Gateway's report card. Is your equipment functioning properly? Meeting your needs? Invoiced correctly? And perhaps most important, what was the courtesy level of our personnel?"

Weekly survey reports go to senior management—the president and chief financial officer—to make sure ". . . we are covering all the bases where our customers are concerned."

Customers often contribute constructive comments that can be incorporated in operations, such as lengthening demonstration time for certain complex products. "Our survey gives customers a chance to exercise their partner role," says Sweet. "Often their comments help us plan future product strategies."

Telemarketing questions, coupled with the service surveys, determine customers' interest level on new products and training, and function as a communications tool—getting the word out quickly on upcoming products. Sweet says this is a customer service as well as an internal Gateway Computer tool because it helps the user plan and budget for future purchases.

Selvage takes the concept one step further: "We never forget that, ultimately, computers are used by people. It is an important part of our responsibility to serve their growth needs as well as the current functions their equipment must perform."

PCM (PROFESSIONAL COMMUNITY MANAGEMENT)

The Towers at the premier retirement community, Leisure World, in Laguna Hills. Leisure World has been managed by PCM since its inception.

It's a well-known fact that Americans are living longer and taking their leisure earlier these days than in generations past. Add to that the pleasant Southern California environment, and you have some of the reasons for the outstanding success of Leisure World, the premier retirement community in Laguna Hills.

Much can also be attributed to PCM (Professional Community Management), the management company that oversees the operations of this 1,600-acre, 22,000-resident community in South Orange County. PCM, founded in 1972 after an eight-year association on site of the retirement community, offers a wide range of services, including financial, personnel, maintenance, and recreation, and provides the general management expertise for the efficient operation of the beautiful community.

PCM, based in nearby El Toro, is a subsidiary of Retirement Living Affiliates (RLA) and a division of Affiliates Group, Inc. (AGI). Its clients include a variety of communities for residents of all ages, from singles and young families to senior residents. PCM has received national recognition as a proven leader in the management of retirement housing and community associations.

PCM manages approximately 30,000 units in Orange, San Diego, Riverside, and Los Angeles counties in communities that vary in size from 100 to 12,700 units. Leisure World in Laguna Hills is the largest and one of the most prestigious communities under the firm's management. PCM is one of Orange County's largest employers with about 1,100 workers.

PCM and RLA also specialize in the development and management of congregated living facilities. These residences for senior adults feature a complete host of amenities and services such as complete housekeeping, maintenance, social activities, and a choice of one to three meals each day in attractive restaurant-style dining rooms.

Real estate brokerage is an integral part of PCM's business, too. Through PCM Realty and Marketing, PCM/Laguna Hills Resales, and Sears Realty, clients are

A typical family-oriented PCM-managed community.

served in the selling of their homes.

Even though PCM has become a large operation, it continually emphasizes its personal commitment to management excellence. This excellence is reflected in a highly skilled team of management professionals who are dedicated to servicing the individual needs of each community. Through its professional management services, PCM contributes greatly to the life-style of its clients.

PCM and many of its communities have grown up together, with both entities contributing heartily to the economic evolution of Orange County. Volunteer activity is an important part of the firm's philosophy, with president Jeffrey B. Olsen, senior vice-president Russell L. Disbro, and some of their colleagues serving on the board of directors of a hospital, chambers of commerce, local water boards, the United Way, and other community groups.

PCM expects its consultant and management roles to grow along with the population and development, and foresees greater teamwork with builders who create the inviting master-planned communities of tomorrow.

ERNST & WHINNEY

Sophisticated and urban describes Ernst & Whinney's Orange County offices in the impressive Koll Center/Irvine at 18400 Von Karman. The setting and the practice reflect a changed image and a changed marketplace, since the company established its local presence in 1963.

Small-town Santa Ana was a hospitable, about-to-be-discovered host to Ernst & Whinney's first effort in Orange County. Recalls Guy Wilson, now managing partner in the firm's Los Angeles office, "The luncheon club in our

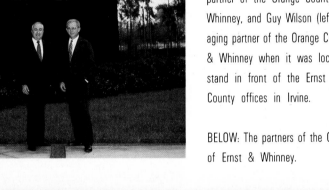

building was practically empty in those days, with three—maybe four patrons. I introduced myself to one of them and we began to lunch together, even though he was a major competitor setting up shop, just as I was."

Ernst & Whinney is now one of the largest professional services firms in the world, with accountants, tax advisers, and management consultants who help clients meet contemporary business challenges and anticipate future needs. The company serves a diverse client base, yet also has built a reputation for specializing in particular growth industries. Clients include more than 14,000 organi-

LEFT: Thomas Testman (right), current managing partner of the Orange County office of Ernst & Whinney, and Guy Wilson (left), the original managing partner of the Orange County office of Ernst & Whinney when it was located in Santa Ana, stand in front of the Ernst & Whinney Orange County offices in Irvine.

BELOW: The partners of the Orange County office of Ernst & Whinney.

zations and thousands of individuals, and comprise approximately 10 percent of the firms registered with the Securities and Exchange Commission. Sixty-five of the largest industrial companies listed on the *Fortune* 500 are among Ernst & Whinney's client ranks, while many others are small enterprises developing promising ideas.

As a firm that earns its fees through helping clients prosper, Ernst & Whinney has made remarkable progress of its own: With 420 offices and 33,000 employees in 75 countries, its worldwide revenues are $1.5 billion. U.S. employees number 13,000 in 117 offices, including national headquarters in Cleveland, Ohio.

Its Orange County work force currently numbers 150, with 12 partners in the Irvine/Newport Beach office. Growth has been especially dramatic since 1980, when Ernst & Whinney moved to Newport Beach under the auspices of new managing partner Thomas Testman. "Management decided to establish a presence in the industries and businesses destined for growth," Testman explains. "We consciously sought to grow in specialty areas that paralleled the county's own spectacular development."

Among the most promising fields: health care, real estate, entrepreneurial, and international business. Among the most needed additional services: new technologies, broad business consultation, and creative financing advice.

Given Orange County's burgeoning activity in medical technology and Testman's own depth of experience in the health care field, it is no surprise that Ernst & Whinney has emerged as a leading service firm to that growth industry. Just as A.C. Ernst, who founded the company in 1903, is credited with having done much to define modern accounting and consulting practice, so are Ernst & Whinney professionals touted for breaking new ground in a revolutionized health care field.

In Orange County, as in the nation, great technological and scientific advancements—driven by the information explosion—are taking place in health care. Add to that major changes from government on the nation's cost reimbursement system, and there is a whole new need for professional support services.

Ernst & Whinney focused on that technical need by creating a new specialty department. Staff members study the client's technical business as avidly as if their own, to provide value in areas other than accounting. Firm officials stay visibly involved with universities to help foster interaction between academia and the business community. At the University of California, Irvine, for instance, Ernst & Whinney helped found the Corporate University Partner Program (CUPP) for communication relating to technology transfer.

The same department strategy has worked well in other areas, too. Several years ago there was limited real estate experience at Ernst & Whinney; now there are 25 accountants and tax experts who are conversant in the nuances of commercial, industrial, and residential transactions. Firm leaders point to the group's cohesiveness and team focus as key factors for success.

Management consulting services, which cover a broad range of industries, may include designing a new computer control system, advising a chief executive on a potential acquisition, or helping a new firm with early funding. Ernst & Whinney's Western Re-

gion designates Orange County its headquarters for this specialty.

On the international scene, the firm uses its worldwide resources liberally for the client's advantage. As economic environments become increasingly complex at home and abroad, this capability has become a more important service. In Orange County, the influx of international visitors considering the area for economic development has given new impetus to the firm's foreign influence.

Local community needs still draw the greatest interest, support, and participation from Ernst & Whinney employees. Social programs, service clubs, the arts, and politics rate high on their list. Managing partner Testman, as immediate past chairman of the Industrial League of Orange County, has dealt with important regional issues such as transportation ". . . to work for the good of all commerce. We must upgrade our current infrastructure to maintain our quality of life."

The firm personality is said to reflect each office. In Orange County, the entrepreneurial spirit does predominate, in keeping with

the way most Orange County clients do business. But the local office does join hands with its global network to provide extensive programs and resources for both employees and clients.

In operating as a worldwide partnership, Ernst & Whinney encourages its professionals to act as catalysts for progress by bringing the right people and the right ideas together. The Orange County office—with its emphasis on high quality and youthful living—maintains an abundance of resources eager to help move the firm's goals forward.

The lobby (above, right) and exterior (right) of Ernst & Whinney's Orange County offices at 18400 Von Karman in the Koll Center in Irvine.

FRED. S. JAMES & CO. OF CALIFORNIA, INC.

It's not often that a complex topic such as insurance is characterized as exciting and creative. But that's the way senior vice-president Roger E. Clayton describes day-to-day activity at the Fred. S. James & Co. office he oversees in Irvine.

James/Irvine, Orange County's largest insurance broker, grew from 15th to third in nationwide company branch rankings for total commissions and fees during the past several years. Clayton attributes the outstanding growth to an aggressive management team, an inspired staff, and the county's dynamic and diversified economy. "We are a full-service brokerage with specialists on staff locally to meet our clients' needs and the changing nature of the industry," Clayton notes.

James/Irvine's basic services beyond insurance brokerage encompass risk management, actuarial services, and employee benefit consulting for a variety of industries. Developers and retail companies are prominent on the firm's key client list.

Staff specialties at Fred. S. James & Co. have been fueled by several emerging trends in the marketplace: the increasing need for self-insurance and risk management, the emphasis on employee benefit programs, and the development of Pacific Rim trade influence at home and abroad.

As the end of the century nears, experts anticipate a greater percentage of insurance dollars will be spent to cover risk at self-insured levels. Corporate mergers are expected to continue, creating a greater need for innovative insurance concepts. James/Irvine devotes several full-time positions to providing this professional expertise.

Employee benefits, a major part of any company's payroll in today's economy, are an important service at James. More than a dozen people cover the complex field for clients, with services ranging from workers' compensation and pension plans to deferred compensation and employee communications.

The continued influx of Pacific Rim business to Orange County has influenced the firm to offer more offshore programs, as well as multinational and international insurance consulting. This is a natural outgrowth of Fred. S. James & Co.'s relationship as the North American operating unit of its parent, the London-based Sedgwick Group plc, the second-largest insurance brokerage in the world. Sedgwick's acquisition of James in 1985 strengthened both units' bid for greater global representation with a network of seasoned insurance professionals. The Sedgwick Group has more than 300 offices in 64 countries and some 15,000 employees worldwide.

The original Fred. S. James & Co. was established in Chicago in 1858. Through acquisitions the firm spread its full-service concept throughout the nation. It purchased the former Peacock Insurance Agency with its 25 employees in Laguna Beach in 1972. The Irvine office, established in 1978, consolidated Peacock with other acquisitions and has grown to more than 150 employees housed in 40,000 square feet, on two full floors of Koll Center Irvine, at 18201 Von Karman.

BELOW LEFT: Fred. S. James & Co.'s new offices are housed in one of Orange County's most recognizable and innovatively designed structures—Koll Center, overlooking the San Diego Freeway.

BELOW: Occupying the entire seventh and eighth floors, the James/Irvine staff of more than 150 employees represents only a small fraction of Fred. S. James' 39-office, 4,600-employee network.

BUILDING GREATER ORANGE COUNTY

From concept to completion, Orange County's construction industry shapes tomorrow's skyline.

Coto de Caza, 162-163

The Tishman West Management Corporation/The City, 164-165

C.J. Segerstrom & Sons, 166

Orange County is constantly changing its face with the construction of new office buildings and housing tracts. Photo by Yana Bridle

COTO DE CAZA

Coto de Caza—meaning preserve of the hunt—is true to its name, whether in Portuguese or English. Coto, until recently a remote and undeveloped valley near mountain wilderness, has kept its natural terrain intact while becoming an exclusive ranch-style community with modern-day comforts.

The rustic Coto gained world-wide recognition when it hosted the 1984 Olympic Games' Modern Pentathlon at its highly reputed equestrian center. But as a master-planned community that develops not only dwellings but life-styles, Coto de Caza is just beginning to make its mark.

One of the largest private residential developments in Southern California, Coto is in southeast Orange County, south of El Toro and east of Mission Viejo. It is set in a tranquil valley approximately six miles long and one mile wide, and it shares some of Trabuco Canyon's hillsides as well as views of the Saddleback Mountains.

Historically the area has been remote, largely owing to limited road access. Now it is only some 30 minutes away from John Wayne Airport, thanks to the newly constructed Santa Margarita Parkway, and a hillside away from the new schools, major shopping, and commercial centers in nearby Rancho Santa Margarita.

Coto de Caza, a billion-dollar project that already boasts a championship golf course and the famous Vic Braden Tennis College, is a joint development of Arvida/JMB Partners and Chevron Land and Development Company. The dual effort got its start in the mid-1980s, refueling what had been a leisurely development mode for Coto.

In the late 1800s Coto was part of the massive Rancho Santa Margarita. Over the years it was sold to other family ranchos, and remained a sleepy inland property until 1969, when a group of private investors and Great Southwest, the real estate subsidiary of Penn Central Railroad, started development. After Penn Central's much publicized bankruptcy in the early 1970s, the Coto master plan was temporarily halted, though later transferred to Great Southwest's sister company, Arvida.

The change was fortunate for Coto because Arvida/JMB Partners, as a premier Florida developer, has produced many outstanding recreational properties. Among them are the Longboat Key Club and Boca West in Florida.

Arvida/JMB Partners is the managing partner of the development. Chevron Land, a subsidiary of Chevron Corporation, contributes longtime experience in California development and substantial stability from its corporate parent to complement the partnership.

The Coto de Caza of the late 1980s is developing as a haven for primary home buyers, although an estimated 20 percent of the new residents will be second-home owners who want a getaway atmosphere with complete recreational conveniences. The low-density construction, with a proposed average of 1.2 homes per acre, offers single-family homes, town houses, and patio

ABOVE: Coto de Caza's new private 18-hole golf course, designed by Robert Trent Jones, Jr., is open seven days a week for play.

LEFT: The Vic Braden Tennis College offers comprehensive instruction for beginners and advanced players, with six color-coded instructional courts and 17 geometric teaching lanes.

homes catering to all age groups. In 10 to 15 years Coto's 4,000 acres will host up to approximately 6,000 residential units. Some of Southern California's leading builders are involved in the project: Pacesetter Homes, Gfeller Development Co., and J.M. Peters Co.

One of the very special features in Coto's sports retinue is Vic Braden's Tennis College. Braden, the tennis guru known for his lighthearted approach to teaching, also puts a high-technology spin on his instruction. He videotapes students on the court, then uses instant replay in the classroom to teach better form.

The 18-hole golf course, said to contain all the elements necessary to attract the game's greatest players, has preserved Coto's natural terrain admirably. Designer Robert Trent Jones, Jr., who also designed the Monterey Peninsula's Spyglass Hill and many others, allowed 200-year-old oak trees to ring several greens and an ancient stand of willows to line several fairways. *USA Today* ranked Coto as one of the top five courses built in California since 1962.

Coto's equestrian center has attracted many residents who like having organized trail rides, bullpen jump chutes, boarding facilities, and riding instruction

available.

There are general-interest recreational facilities on the premises as well, including a fitness center with swimming, racquetball, bowling, basketball, volleyball, and trap and skeet shooting. Use of the private club facilities is not included in the price of a lot or home.

In keeping with its wilderness image, Coto's master plan is committed to preserving more than one-third of its acreage. Five hundred acres have already been donated to the County Wagon Wheel Regional Park in the southern part of the valley. With the Cleveland National Forest and National Audubon Society's Starr Ranch Wildlife Sanctuary bordering the valley, home owners will have a scenic and serene back-

drop. Perhaps it is thanks to this preservation of open space that Coto has been called the Beverly Hills of Orange County.

The developers are working closely with environmental regulatory agencies to document the plants, birds, and animals that share the valley to keep a natural balance. To that end Chevron Land's sister subsidiary, Chevron USA, is funding extensive wildlife studies—such as the mountain lion ecology study—through Audubon to learn how animal populations can be preserved and coexist with the growing human population.

By caring for twentieth-century creatures as well as comforts, Coto de Caza's master planners hope to establish an environmental standard that will endure for future generations.

ABOVE: Coto de Caza's exclusive communities with some homesites that provide a unique perspective of the course and valley below to a panorama of rolling hills and a striking ridgeline.

LEFT: Many of Coto de Caza's homesites are zoned for horses. Individual or group trail rides are available at the Coto de Caza Equestrian Center, one of the finest facilities in California.

THE TISHMAN WEST MANAGEMENT CORPORATION/THE CITY

The City, in the city of Orange in central Orange County, clearly is an easy place to find. The imposing mixed-use business community in the 174-acre complex, called a city within a city, is in the heart of a freeway network that includes the Santa Ana (5), Garden Grove (22), and Orange (57), and is near four other freeways that lead to points north and east.

The complex is a joint venture of Metropolitan Life Insurance Company and Tishman West Management Corp. When it opened in 1970, it was the first such development in the central county. It still is the largest mixed-use development there, and includes commercial office space, retail shops, entertainment and dining establish-

The City is a mixed-use complex on 174 acres in the city of Orange. A joint venture between Metropolitan Life Insurance Company and Tishman West Management Corp., The City includes commercial and office space, retail shops, entertainment and dining establishments, service facilities, and residential apartments.

ments, service facilities, and even residential apartments. Not surprisingly, The City, with its central location, is home to the Orange County Chamber of Commerce.

The City has attracted top firms from all over the country. It has grown into one of the largest business communities countywide—

no mean feat with the recent construction explosion—and has more than 1.5 million square feet of office space in nine low-, mid-, and high-rise buildings. In recent years The City added a hotel, the 460-room Doubletree Inn, with meeting and conference facilities.

The partners chose Doubletree

Inns Inc. to manage the hotel because the Phoenix-based firm is experienced at handling business-oriented traffic and is knowledgeable about marketing hotels that are near recreational facilities. Indeed, the hotel is a decided plus for tenants in nearby office buildings who need amenities for meetings or out-of-town visitors.

While the Doubletree Inn specializes in business guests' needs, it also draws the tourist trade because of several famous attractions in its own backyard: Disneyland, Anaheim Stadium, and the Crystal Cathedral. Of course the Anaheim Convention Center, also in the neighborhood, is a draw for the business visitor. Within the hotel, the top floor has been set aside for executive suites, so popular among corporate leaders.

The newest addition to The City is The City Tower, a $65-million, 20-story office building that is the tallest in central Orange County. Completed in late 1987, the tower also offers a six-level parking structure that accommodates 1,450 vehicles.

Designed by Daniel L. Dworsky Architect & Associates, FAIA, the same firm that designed several other buildings in the complex, the tower adds 410,000 rentable square feet to The City. The reflective glass building in shades of blue and gray was planned to enhance its natural surroundings, while incorporating the most contemporary efficiencies. The reflective glass repeats the theme used in some of the other City structures.

Tishman, one of California's largest diversified commercial developers, is manager, leasing agent, and developer of this complex. Recently the company was listed as the 14th largest nationwide among privately held companies by *Building Design and Construction* magazine. The firm's professionals have designed, built, leased, and managed major real estate development projects throughout the nation.

The company's financial partner, Metropolitan Life, is one of the nation's largest insurance and financial services firms, and one of the largest institutional investors, with more than $800 million in real estate investments in the Los Angeles area alone.

Officials from both companies acknowlege that the joint-venture produces advantages for all concerned. It allows each partner to expand and handle more of a project than as a party of one. It produces a strengthened position in meeting the competition as well.

Much of The City's success has been attributed to Perry S. Herst, Jr., Tishman's president. Under his guidance, The City prospered into the complex that it is today. Until the ground breaking for The City Tower, Herst could only offer potential tenants a long waiting list position, because of the development's popularity and unavailability of space.

Herst, who became Tishman's president in 1977, had spearheaded the successful development of Chicago's $100-million Gateway Center. His early vision for Orange County has become a reality with the growth of The City.

In Tishman's and Metropolitan Life's joint-venture, demographics figured prominently in the master planning. A half-million people live within five miles of the project, comprising not only a diversified labor pool but a growing consumer base for the shopping mall. Corporate tenants who located in this burgeoning commercial corridor include a number of blue-chip companies. Among the largest tenants are Bank of America and TRW.

The regional shopping center, at the core of the complex, is an enclosed mall anchored by two major department stores, JCPenney and The May Company. More than 100 stores, restaurants, theaters, and other services are available at The City, with restaurants that cater primarily to the large number of office workers at the project.

Tishman has been developer of The City since 1974. Currently the company is developing and managing more than 16 million square feet of commercial and retail space throughout the western United States, including Denver, Phoenix, San Francisco, San Diego, and Los Angeles. Tishman operates on site as a leasing and management agent, and as such is in a better position to offer tenants an oversight to their needs. "We're bullish on the city of Orange," Herst notes. "It has an outstanding location, straddling the freeway system as it does, so important in our Southern California society."

The City is a prime example of a project that has been developed through the natural progression of a master plan. Cohesiveness through landscaping, building access, walkways, and roadways serves the pedestrian and motorist equally.

The City Tower, a $65-million, 20-story office building, is the newest addition and the tallest building in central Orange County. Completed in late 1987, the tower also offers a six-level parking structure that accommodates 1,450 vehicles.

C.J. SEGERSTROM & SONS

If "urban village" sounds like a contradictory term, one need only visit South Coast Plaza and its neighboring Town Center in Costa Mesa to know the description is apt. Contemporary, compact, and convenient, the metropolitan complex blends commerce and culture, luxury and necessity.

Town Center's gradual urbanization has been called a sociocultural phenomenon because it has combined elements in a mixed-use setting that didn't seem compatible: office buildings with performing arts centers, shopping malls with fine dining. But the combination has proved to be an unqualified success and a source of synergy that has given central Orange County a recognizable metropolitan focus with significant economic interplay among the participating businesses.

South Coast Plaza, America's premier retail center, has become a major tourist destination with sales rivaling the two leading retail centers in the state of California—Rodeo Drive in Beverly Hills and San Francisco. Its specialty shops, sidewalk cafes, ethnic restaurants, and lush indoor landscaping attract kings and ambassadors as well as regional shoppers. Adjacent to many of the world's finest stores and upscale gourmet restaurants, the Orange County Performing Arts Center, South Coast Repertory Theater, Westin South Coast Plaza Hotel, South Coast Plaza Village, and more fine restaurants have been the focus of national attention by both the print and broadcast media as well as a magnet for major business investment in the area.

C.J. Segerstrom & Sons, the real estate partnership that developed today's urban village, has been praised by civic leaders for being sensitive to fine art and culture in creating a balanced community. The Segerstroms have been prominent in Orange County since the turn of the century, pioneering

both agricultural and commercial interests.

The family opened South Coast Plaza in March 1967 as Orange County's first enclosed regional shopping center. With the addition of Crystal Court with flagship anchors J.W. Robinson and The Broadway in 1986 and additional specialty stores and boutiques, gross sales in 1987 were more than $650 million. South Coast Plaza has a long list of distinguished retailers that includes eight major department and specialty stores with merchandise

that favors the entire spectrum of shopper interest.

Town Center was planned with pedestrian appeal, an oddity in Southern California. With the hotel as its nucleus, this 77-acre, master-planned center includes banks, office buildings, and world-renowned sculptures by Henry Moore, Joan Miro, and Isamu Noguchi all within walking distance of the plaza.

The two-year-old Performing Arts Center, with its 3,000-seat Segerstrom Hall, has drawn interna-

ABOVE: Crystal Court at South Coast Plaza opened in 1986. The three-level area added two major department stores and 70 specialty stores and restaurants.

LEFT: The 21-story, 465,000-square-foot Center Tower in Town Center is one of Orange County's newest and finest office buildings. It features polished Napoleon Red Swedish granite and solar gray glass.

tional touring productions of musical theater, symphony, opera, and dance from its inception.

Next-door-neighbor South Coast Repertory, a professional resident theater company for 23 years, opened there in 1978. Nationally known for its innovative programming of classic and contemporary plays, South Coast Repertory is truly an urbane addition to the once-little village with city tastes.

QUALITY OF LIFE

Medical and educational institutions contribute to the security and intellectual development of Orange County area residents.

Hoag Memorial Hospital Presbyterian, 168-169

Martin Luther Hospital, 170-171

Shiley Incorporated, 172-173

Anaheim Memorial Hospital, 174

United Way of Orange County, 175

California Angels, 176

HOAG MEMORIAL HOSPITAL PRESBYTERIAN

Since its founding more than three decades ago, Hoag Memorial Hospital Presbyterian has experienced exceptional, uninterrupted growth, along with the communities surrounding it. Today, from its vantage point high on the bluff overlooking Newport Harbor, Hoag continues building—facilities, programs, technologies, and, more important, an outstanding staff—to meet the hospital's commitment to the health care needs of its community. This Hoag commitment is strengthened by the fact that it is a two-way commitment, for it is the charitable support of Hoag's community that provides the margin needed to generate the hospital's outstanding growth.

One of the largest medical centers in Orange County, Hoag is licensed for 471 beds, more than 2,000 employees, a medical staff of over 600 physicians, and an operating budget of more than $170 million. Serving as the foundation for the hospital's reputation for quality patient care is a staff of physicians, nurses, technicians, therapists, counselors, and other health care professionals whose expertise and caring translate the millions of dollars worth of facilities and equipment into the highest-quality care available for every individual patient.

As Hoag's growth and expansion continue, the hospital has refurbished several existing areas, while constructing new space for other special disciplines. Included are construction of an $18-million free-standing outpatient cancer center; establishment of a heart transplant program; total renovation of the childbirth center, with construction of innovative labor/delivery/recovery rooms; refurbishment of space to house a chemical dependency center; construction of a new magnetic resonance imaging diagnostic center; construction of a satellite health center in the community of Irvine; and construction of a new hospital entrance for the convenience of outpatients and visitors.

A vital part of Hoag's role as the leading provider of cancer care to county residents, the new George and Patricia Hoag Cancer Center is the first facility of its kind in Orange County, dedicated solely to the needs of cancer patients who require outpatient treatment. Currently under construction, the center brings together all the human and technological resources currently available to fight this dreaded disease.

Located adjacent to the hospital, the three-story, 65,000-square-foot center centralizes diagnosis, treatment, and research in one easily accessible location. A large area of the center is devoted to radia-

LEFT: Ground breaking for Hoag Memorial Hospital took place more than three decades ago on the bluff overlooking Newport Harbor.

ABOVE: One of Hoag Memorial's new labor, delivery, and recovery (LDR) rooms.

tion therapy, along with a day hospital for chemotherapy treatment. Other features include capabilities for hyperthermia, a promising new treatment that uses heat to help destroy cancer cells; a tumor registry for important national research data gathering; classrooms; laboratories; offices for teams of cancer specialists and support staff; and a small cafeteria.

Changing times have had a dramatic impact upon another important area of Hoag. Today the Hoag Childbirth Center has a totally different look following extensive refurbishment to create innovative LDR (labor/delivery/recovery) rooms for new mothers. Labor, delivery, and recovery all take place in one room—a very special room that looks like a beautifully designed room at home rather than a hospital room. New mothers, along with their doctors, decide who will be present during their birth experience, as well as how they will care for the baby after its birth.

The Hoag Childbirth Center also includes one of the area's most comprehensive education programs, as well as a nationally recognized fertility program, a highly specialized perinatology service for high-risk mothers, and an advanced neonatal intensive care nursery.

Another recently renovated area on the Hoag Hospital campus houses a program of special care for special patients. The Hoag Chemical Dependency Center, with 21 beds for inpatients, offers help and hope to both patients and their families in a beautiful, nonthreatening environment. Patients undergo an intensive three-week inpatient treatment program, which includes extensive counseling for family members as well as patients. A 12-month after-care program is included as part of the treatment.

Reflecting Hoag's commitment to making science's most advanced technology available to the community today, the hospital's new Magnetic Resonance Imaging Center houses a powerful, noninvasive scanner that allows doctors to look inside the body with clarity and detail not previously available. Remarkable computer technology visualizes the body's internal structures for a wide variety of studies and applications.

As Hoag has continued to grow and develop, so have the communities surrounding it. One of the fastest growing is Irvine, home to nearly 100,000 residents, more of whom have traditionally looked to Hoag than any other hospital for their health care. When Hoag Health Center-Irvine opened its doors recently, the facilities and services it offered were the first, most comprehensive of their kind in the area. The three-story, 33,000-square-foot center houses private physicians' offices, an urgent care center for minor medical emergencies, a women's health center, an imaging center, a health

LEFT: A model of the new Cancer Center, the first facility of its kind in Orange County dedicated solely to the needs of cancer patients who require outpatient treatment.

ABOVE: An aerial view of Hoag Memorial Hospital—one of the largest and most advanced medical centers in Orange County.

resource library, and one of the most comprehensive community education programs in Orange County.

The expansion of facilities, the continually developing programs, and the nationally recognized medical staff—all are testimony to the strength of a commitment dating back to 1944. That was the year Reverend Raymond Brahams, disturbed by the increasing number of injuries on the treacherous coast highway and lack of a nearby medical facility, organized a group to build a hospital for coastal residents. Braham's group —seven Presbyterian Church members and a physician—began raising funds for the new hospital by enlisting church and private support.

Fortuitously, the Hoag Foundation, established in 1940 by George Grant Hoag, Sr., his wife Grace, and their son, George Hoag II, was searching for a worthwhile project to honor the memory of its founder. It was the Hoag Foundation that provided the funding needed to complete Reverend Braham's hospital project. Thus began a lifelong association between the Hoag family and the hospital destined to provide health care for a vast coastal community of Orange County.

Thus the hospital that began in 1952 with 75 beds has expanded along with the community it serves. Plans for the future are perhaps best expressed by Hoag Hospital president Michael Stephens: "The progress made at Hoag over the past years reflects a great deal of change. One thing, however, will never change—the Hoag commitment to provide residents of Orange County with the highest level of patient care. That commitment has guided Hoag Hospital from its inception, and it will continue to do so in the years to come."

MARTIN LUTHER HOSPITAL

Care, respect, responsiveness—this credo has served Martin Luther Hospital well as it nears three decades as a community hospital. The hospital, a fully accredited, not-for-profit institution, serves patients in north Orange County from its Anaheim location at 1830 West Romneya Drive.

From the very beginning MLH gained a reputation as an innovator and model health care practitioner, while maintaining a friendly atmosphere and personal touch. As a 200-bed hospital with 800 employees, MLH is considered medium sized. Yet it requires 40 departments to conduct all its services, direct its $65-million annual budget, and develop forward-thinking programs to meet society's needs.

The hospital's sense of community is a strong recurring theme throughout its programs. Among the best known is R.E.A.C.H., or Resources for Employee Assistance and Comprehensive Health, which was started in 1980 for its own staff, then expanded to serve the public. MLH provides counseling and referrals to employees and their families from participating firms in a variety of industries, including electronics, municipalities, manufacturing, and publishing.

Counselors address problems related to alcohol, marriage, jobs, family, stress, drugs, finance, health, and legal matters.

A highly visible community health program—sports medicine and rehabilitation—has closely paralleled the nation's physical fitness mania for the past six years. Experts treat tennis elbows and joggers' knees, as well as the more serious ailments, and work closely with school athletic teams to help prevent injuries through better education.

The community has easy access to MLH through several telephone programs: Tel-Med and Tel-Hospital, educational audio tape libraries that offer three- to five-minute discourses on a variety of vital medical topics. Tel-Med addresses specific subjects on disease, diet, and public information. Tel-Hospital is geared to tests and procedures for those about to be admitted for treatment. Listeners can access the tapes free of charge simply by calling a toll-free number from the privacy of their home telephone. Through a subscription service called Lifeline®, the disabled or elderly can call for help through an automatic dialing

ABOVE: Community service is at the heart of Anaheim-based Martin Luther Hospital programs. The center has a history of continuing growth in both innovative technologies and physical plant.

LEFT: Neighbors Mickey and Minnie Mouse from nearby Disneyland frequently help out with the center's health fairs.

system that connects with the hospital's emergency department.

The hospital goes into the community through its extensive speakers' bureau. Health and wellness are the issues at hand, as well as practical explanations of pricing and government's role in health care. The speakers are experts who can address topics of interest for every age group.

This growing interaction between hospital and community is also manifest between hospital and doctors, dictated by economic facts in the health care field today. It is a conscious cooperative effort—even partnership—to control costs while funding expensive new technology and equipment. At MLH there is now a full-time staff member dedicated to building and maintaining viable practices for the 500 physicians affiliated with the hospital.

One of the hospital's newer capabilities, which opened recently, is a pediatric department. It is a natural extension of its busy obstetrics department and its five-year-old special-care nursery, which was the first in the county to be licensed for intermediate-level, intensive neonatal care for infants.

And there are other innovations. The newly configured Outpatient Pavilion has grown from 4,000 to 6,000 square feet, and includes an outpatient surgery center. With its own entrance, lobby, registration, and parking, the pavilion offers patients convenience as well as economy.

ABOVE RIGHT: More than 200 babies per month see their first light at MLH—as births and special nursery care are important specialties.

RIGHT: The hospital's state-of-the-art equipment in current diagnostic radiology includes this digital subtraction angiography unit.

MLH has broadened its functional scope by becoming a full founding member of LHS Corp., a nonprofit, multihospital, parent company based in Los Angeles. The linkage provides access to a network of experts in fields such as financial analysis, information systems, management services, and others.

The shared-services concept also enabled the hospital to join with a group of its medical staff to purchase a state-of-the-art CT scan for a substantial investment. Future plans call for such cooperation to flourish, to meet the dynamics of an ever-changing health care field.

The hospital has been well served by an $800,000 Kellogg Foundation Grant in which it participated several years ago. By studying successful marketing skills used in business and industry over a period of three years, and adapting them to hospital needs, MLH has made great strides as an industry leader. It was one of seven hospitals chosen from 300 nationwide to participate, and its personnel studied such diverse groups as hotels, airlines, and banks.

MLH's leadership stance was clearly established in 1960 when it became the first voluntary hospital in the county to provide radiation therapy, using cobalt as a source, in treating cancer. In 1973 the center pioneered a hemodialysis unit, an external kidney machine that purifies the blood of the patient with kidney failure.

Martin Luther Hospital is governed by two volunteer groups: a board of directors and a foundation board. Although it has no tie with the Lutheran Church, as its name would suggest, the hospital's inception stemmed from a group of Lutheran ministers in the community who saw a need for another medical facility and helped activate the project. Speculation has it that the founders, who represented a number of denominations, chose the traditional name to convey stability and trustworthiness—a reputation that is still cultivated very carefully.

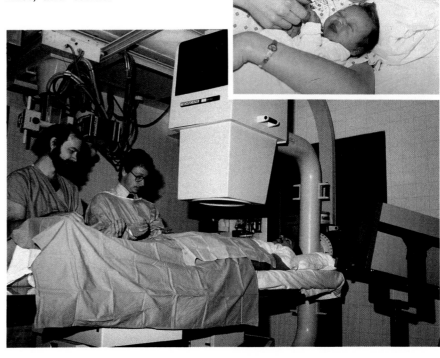

SHILEY INCORPORATED

Shiley Incorporated began two short decades ago through the talent and individual initiative of founder Donald P. Shiley, who developed a new design for a disc-type artificial heart valve. Its success led to the development of a more advanced tilting disc valve that set a new standard for the industry and launched a company that has grown to become a worldwide leader in the medical device field.

During the 1970s Shiley started producing tracheostomy tubes and introduced a patented blood oxygenator for use in open heart surgery. As these product lines gained widespread market acceptance, Shiley's facilities expanded into the company's present 300,000-square-foot headquarters complex in Irvine. Meanwhile, the total number of employees soared from about 40 people in 1970 to nearly 2,300 in 16 facilities around the world today. Annual sales have multiplied fourfold from $50 million in 1979 to more than $200 million in 1987.

In 1979 Shiley became a wholly owned subsidiary of Pfizer Inc., a research-based firm headquartered in New York, with worldwide businesses in health care, agriculture, specialty chemicals, materials science, and consumer products. Shiley is one of the largest members of Pfizer's Hospital Products Group.

From its inception, Shiley Incorporated fulfilled a significant business purpose: to provide the best-possible products to serve the needs of cardiac surgeons and patients. Growth and product diversification over the years have enabled Shiley to broaden that purpose into developing and producing sophisticated medical devices for use not only by surgeons, but also by other medical professionals in a widening range of specialties.

Today Shiley is a developer, manufacturer, and marketer of

The main building of Shiley's Irvine headquarters complex. Founded as a single product company in 1966, Shiley has since grown to worldwide prominence in the medical device industry.

medical devices in the cardiopulmonary, cardiovascular, and critical care areas. Shiley's product list is long and impressive: mechanical heart valves to restore the vital pulse of blood through the body, tracheostomy tubes that supply the breath of life to patients of all ages, vascular access products used in life-saving hemodialysis procedures, blood oxygenators and pumps that function as the patient's heart and lungs during open heart surgery, implantable infusion pumps that automatically deliver medication directly where and when it's most needed, diagnostic and interventional cardiology and radiology catheters enabling surgeons to examine and clear blocked arteries, and autotransfusion equipment enabling patients to receive transfusions of their own blood during surgery.

Shiley has recently entered the dynamic field of cardiology, radiology, and angioplasty catheters. These products support new, less invasive techniques used to treat cardiovascular disease, often avoiding or delaying bypass surgery through angioplasty, a procedure in which a small catheter is carefully inserted into a coronary artery that has become blocked with plaque. A tiny balloon at the end of the catheter is then inflated, flattening the plaque against the walls of the artery and allowing blood to flow through. These cost-effective devices represent one of the most rapidly growing segments of the medical device market.

Progressing with innovative concepts in medicine, Shiley now provides the only implantable drug delivery system approved by the Food and Drug Administration for sale in the United States. This remarkable electromechanical device is designed to infuse balanced amounts of medication within a patient's body on a preprogrammed basis and has many potential drug therapy applications, including the treatment of diabetes and cancer.

Yet another unprecedented new product area for Shiley consists of autotransfusion devices that are used to cleanse and recycle a patient's own blood before or during surgery, thus reducing the need for transfusions of donor blood and minimizing the risk of transmission of such diseases as hepatitis or AIDS. This product, which is equipped with microprocessor controls, addresses an important medical issue of increasing concern to surgeons and patients. High market potential for the autotransfusion system exists in many diverse medical procedures.

ABOVE: Shiley Tracheostomy Tubes being assembled in a cleanroom. Employee training and certification, and meticulous quality-control procedures ensure production of the highest standards.

RIGHT: Shiley's M2000 Blood Oxygenator undergoes stringent laboratory testing as part of continual research and development efforts geared toward product improvement.

FAR RIGHT: This autotransfusion unit cleanses and returns a patient's blood to him during the course of surgery, minimizing exposure to viral infections by reducing the need for transfusions of donor blood.

Shiley's outstanding growth stems from careful strategic planning that called for both internal product development and expansion through acquisitions that have extended the company's base of operations far beyond Orange County. Recently Shiley acquired several small firms with unique medical products and strong technological capabilities whose locations include Massachusetts, Minnesota, West Germany, Switzerland, and Italy. These newer operations complement Shiley's network of sales offices in all major European countries, as well as in Canada and Australia. Future new product areas and potential acquisitions are continuously being evaluated as part of the company's long-range business development effort, intended to lead the way to further expansion and diversification.

Because Shiley's business took root during Orange County's watershed period of growth, the firm

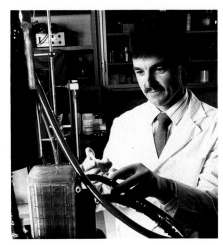

has played an active role in helping to strengthen the local economy and in supporting the community by contributing to the civic and cultural programs that make Orange County exceptional.

However, Shiley possesses a distinctly international identity, evident in the striking array of flags adorning its Irvine facility. More than half of its annual sales take place internationally, making Shiley a partner in health care for surgeons and hospitals worldwide.

A common language shared by Shiley employees worldwide is caring—caring about the integrity of Shiley products and the well-being of patients everywhere who are treated with them. This attitude is reinforced through employee training and certification and manifested in the company's meticulous quality-control procedures.

The entrepreneurial spirit that characterized Shiley in the early days remains in the company's con-temporary research and development activity and approach to the future. Management calls research the lifeblood of the organization, especially in light of the swiftly evolving nature of medical technology. Tomorrow's medical devices are already taking shape in the minds of clinical researchers. To stay on the cutting edge of biomedical engineering and industry advances, Shiley emphasizes continual research and development efforts that respond directly to the clinical experience and needs of physicians, surgeons, and patients.

Shiley's stability, professional expertise, and maturity, established during the formative years of a dynamic industry, have positioned the company well to compete successfully in ever-changing markets at home and abroad. As Shiley Incorporated commences a third decade of business, the organization has renewed its major commitment to investing resources and energy in the quest to more fully understand and master the complexities of mending the human body.

ANAHEIM MEMORIAL HOSPITAL

The large, mirrored exercise room easily could be mistaken for an inviting health spa—if it were not for the sophisticated cardiac monitoring equipment and the uniformed nurses. Anaheim Memorial Hospital's Cardiac Rehabilitation Center, on the ground floor of its Medical Office Building, is a highly visible part of the HeartCare Center of Orange County, a regional service that has established the institution as a leader in cardiac care.

"More open-heart surgery and heart-related procedures have been done at Anaheim Memorial than at any other hospital in Orange County," says Robert M. Sloane, president and chief executive officer. "We've been pacesetters in the cardiovascular field through our acute care center for critical patients and our integrated team approach for treating the disease."

Teams include occupational and physical therapists, dieticians, pharmacists, psychologists, social services counselors, and sometimes biofeedback specialists to treat stress in heart patients.

Oncology also figures high on Anaheim Memorial's list of specialty services, dating from 1975, when the hospital initiated a

Tumor Registry that led to the establishment of the Oncology Department two years later.

Anaheim Memorial, located at 1111 West La Palma, has grown from a 72-bed hospital in 1958 to a multifocused health care center with 240 beds and a balanced roster of dynamic medical services. The independent, community-owned, not-for-profit institution also provides extensive outpatient services and community outreach programs to aid wellness through preventive medicine. Through blood pressure tests, diabetes education classes, arthritis self-help programs, cardiopulmonary resuscitation for bystanders, and other programs, the staff tries to help people stay out of the hospital.

Employees now number about 1,000, with the medical staff approaching 500. The medical center has become a hub of activity that fosters cooperation among health care professionals and providers,

━━━━━━━━━━

BELOW RIGHT: The Cardiac Rehabilitation Center on the first floor of the Anaheim Memorial Hospital Medical Center office building. The center offers personalized rehabilitative care with state-of-the-art monitoring and exercise technology.

LEFT: One of Anaheim Memorial's acute care center nursing stations. The acute care centers include intensive care and two coronary care units.

area residents, government agencies, payers, and local businesses. In response to greater consumer awareness, Anaheim Memorial's leaders say they are focusing on better access to services and cost effectiveness for all.

Outpatient service is a primary way to do both. By using advanced technology, the medical staff can increase options for outpatient diagnoses and treatment. For example, the Cardiac Rehab Center's 10-year-old program that incorporates the latest techniques allows patients to adapt customized exercise programs for home use after a period of time. Such treatment is intended to improve patients' physical and emotional well-being by restoring them to a productive, active, and satisfying life as soon as possible.

Anaheim Memorial emphasizes its role as a resource center for senior citizens through participation in the GoldenHealth PLUS program. It helps members with confusing Medicare forms, reduces out-of-pocket expenses through discounts on prescription drugs, and provides Senior Health Fairs and self-help lectures.

Future plans call for more emphasis on new technology at Anaheim Memorial, tempered with greater efforts to maintain a user-friendly environment—a blend of "high tech, high touch" that keeps Anaheim Memorial Hospital setting the pace in health care for Orange County.

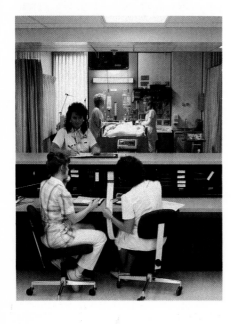

UNITED WAY OF ORANGE COUNTY

One day each year, at the peak of Orange County's beach season, fantasy reigns over reality. In what is called the largest sandcastle competition in the nation, some 1,500 dreamers from local companies and agencies build more than 70 amazing castles and sculptures, to the delight of 18,000 or more spectators who come to see the show. It is a true community event.

The fantasy, sponsored by the United Way of Orange County, helps the organization address the realities of life that exist even in so inviting an area as Orange County: substance abuse, youth problems, cancer and heart disease, homelessness, disability, child abuse, and senior citizens' needs.

For more than a century the United Way has served nationwide as a vehicle to bring community resources and needs together. In Orange County since 1924, the nonprofit group has focused on meeting human care needs through raising and allocating funds, and coordinating services among more than 120 agencies. It has a volunteer board of directors and functions through the support of more than 1,800 companies and thousands of individuals.

Recently the United Way launched a Second Century Initiative, a sweeping plan to meet the dramatic changes taking place in the nation's social fabric: the structure of the American family, the demographic makeup of a growing population, and new single-interest groups with special needs. The 1980s also have introduced heightened competition for funds, a decline in federal funding of social programs, revised tax laws that changed donor deductions, and an American business revolution—with mergers, downsizing, and foreign competition all affecting corporate contributions.

In rethinking tomorrow and beyond, the United Way will not change its mission to increase the organized capacity of people to care for one another. It has modernized its structure, however, to emphasize resource development, marketing, strategic planning and community problem solving, and fund distribution.

The United Way, in its problem-solving capacity, recently sponsored, with several corporations and foundations, a needs assessment survey on top county problems. The ambitious study helped provide direction for all who are working toward creating a better quality of life in Orange County.

Operating as a single communitywide entity, the local United Way conducts a year-round program to enhance its responsiveness to agencies' needs. Its fund-distribution system is more flexible than ever before, allowing donors to choose recipients and know exactly where the funds are going. The system reflects the organization's philosophy of open communications and its desire to cover all demographic bases in the county. Of prime importance is the expanded youth program, designed to help create greater awareness of community needs in a whole new generation of potential volunteers.

The United Way of Orange County and its national parent have set goals to double financial resources and volunteers within the next few years—to meet the ever-needful demands of modern American society.

ABOVE: United Way of Orange County provides funding to 122 local health and human care agencies that serve one out of every four residents.

LEFT: Every September thousands of United Way volunteers carve fantasy sculptures in the sand of Seal Beach to launch the annual fund drive.

CALIFORNIA ANGELS

The little girl in the hospital bed was telling her visitor what the disease was that kept her there. But she was so young, she could hardly pronounce it, and what Don Baylor, then outfielder with the California Angels, heard was "Sixty-Five Roses." That was the start of the California Angels' involvement with Cystic Fibrosis, and the beginning of the Sixty-Five Roses Club that now has support not only from major league baseball teams around the nation, but from football and hockey teams as well.

CF is but one of the many charities the California Angels support in the community that has made the Angels the top-drawing club for attendance in the American League. As an expansion team, however, the Angels had to build fan loyalty from ground zero.

When the team first organized as the Los Angeles Angels in 1961 and played several years in Dodger Stadium, it was still looking for an identity. Management hired a Stanford research group to find the area in California with the best growth potential. All things considered, the Angels chose Orange County.

The Angels christened Anaheim Stadium in 1966—a $24-million structure on 157 acres of land. In their new home, with their new name, the California Angels began building a following that now brings in about 2.7 million spectators a year. "The Big A," the stadium's nickname, taken from its orig-

TOP LEFT: Today the Angels bring in about 2.7 million spectators a year.

TOP RIGHT: Anaheim Stadium is a $24-million structure built on 157 acres of land; it became the home of the Angels in 1966.

RIGHT: Baseball great Reggie Jackson played with the California Angels from 1982 to 1986.

inal A-frame scoreboard, is a comfortable ballpark for fans, and is noted for its cleanliness, friendliness, and safety.

Baseball was a passion of Angels' owner Gene Autry long before he purchased the club. The famous entertainer, known in the early days of radio and cinema as the original Singing Cowboy, has been owner from its inception.

Autry is an American success story himself: As a youth, he bought an eight-dollar guitar from a Sears, Roebuck and Co. mail-order catalog, and parlayed it into a multimillion-dollar business. His spirit and pride in the team have earned him respect and admiration from his players.

It was Autry who encouraged spending on free agents, once the free-agent rule was in place, because he believes the fans deserve to see some big names play. In recent years Reggie Jackson alone cost the Angels organization $3.6 million for four years, a far cry from the $2.1 million Autry paid

for 28 players in 1961.

Yet even in the early years the fledgling Angels scored with some big events: Bo Belinsky's no-hitter in 1962 and Dean Chance's Cy Young Award season in 1964. Then, in 1979, Don Baylor was selected the American League's Most Valuable Player. And recently there have been three division championships in an eight-year period. In 1984, when Reggie Jackson hit his 500th career home run in The Big A, the fans gave him a 15-minute standing ovation.

Autry's philanthropy has set the tone for the club's activity in the community. Players and their families contribute a great deal of time to worthy causes, and the California Angels conduct a strong community recognition program throughout the year.

THE MARKETPLACE

The area's retail establishments, service industries, and products are a mainstay to residents and a magnet to businesses looking to relocate.

Disneyland Hotel, 178-179

Hyatt Regency Alicante Hotel, 180

The Atrium at Newport Center/Fashion Island is a mecca for shoppers. Photo by Yana Bridle

DISNEYLAND HOTEL

The Disneyland Hotel, much like its famous neighbor, is known around the world as a fun place. The resort hotel, whose only formal link to Disneyland is a shared monorail system, provides an oasis—a lush setting with abundant diversions—for guests who want rest and recreation. In recent years it has also become a mecca for the business traveler.

As the Official Hotel of the Magic Kingdom, the hostelry has blossomed from an original 100 rooms into a 1,200-guestroom resort hotel and full-service convention center on 60 acres. The luxurious complex is worth $150 million in facilities and features, and is now one of the most recog-

ABOVE: Disneyland Hotel, a luxurious convention resort on 60 acres in Anaheim, has 1,200 guest rooms. Its 16 restaurants and lounges, along with 160,000 square feet of meeting space, serve both large and small groups.

LEFT: Seaports of the Pacific, a multimillion-dollar playland, includes restaurants with award-winning wines, an international bazaar, pedal boats, and remote-controlled cars on a raceway.

nized and respected hospitality properties in the industry.

The hotel's guest profile, comprised of approximately 60 percent convention trade and 40 percent tourists and families, reflects the growing demand for business-related space. To accommodate its customers' needs the Disneyland Hotel offers 160,000 square feet of meeting rooms, exhibit halls, banquet, and convention space, with most of it under one roof. The hotel regularly hosts very large na-

tional and international groups as well as small local meetings.

The convention facilities in the hotel were planned to create a serious environment for business meetings. But exterior settings and activities are exotic, offering a balance for work and play.

There is an imaginative, 3.5-acre, multimillion-dollar water wonderland called Seaports of the Pacific that captures the fancy of youngsters and adults alike. It includes a 55,000-square-foot inland

marina (23 miles from the ocean), a white-sand beach, waterfalls, and an entertaining display of cascading fountains, lights, and music known as Dancing Waters. Brilliant gardens and distinctive architecture add to the resort aura with a Japanese pagoda, a Balinese temple, and a Chinese junk recreated for visitors.

Sixteen restaurants and lounges, which handle more than one million transactions each year, offer tremendous variety in fare and entertainment. Granville's, the hotel's signature gourmet restaurant and a Travel Holiday Award recipient, is upscale and features 24 unusual glass carvings that depict great mo-

RIGHT: Granville's, an elegant Disneyland Hotel restaurant, has been given a Travel Holiday Award. Its food presentation and unhurried service have made it a favorite for gourmets.

ABOVE: The hotel provides a full range of services for serious business meetings, yet impresses meeting planners with its recreational backdrop for leisure moments.

ments in American history. By contrast, Sgt. Preston's Yukon Saloon and Dancehall offers boisterous fun and lively stage shows.

The Disneyland Hotel has been a success story since its inception in 1954, when Walt Disney asked his friend Jack Wrather to build a hotel adjacent to his new theme park. He had been turned down by Hilton and Sheraton, who were skeptical of building a hotel "in the middle of an orange grove." But Disney had faith in Wrather's entrepreneurial savvy as a wildcatting Texas oilman accustomed to risk taking.

At the time Wrather and his wife, actress/producer Bonita Granville Wrather, also owned several television stations, and produced a number of popular television series and films, among them "Lassie" and "The Lone Ranger."

Their hotel opened in 1955, three months after Disneyland, and has been growing ever since. The 11-story Sierra Tower North, completed in 1961, was Orange County's first high-rise, and the 13-story Bonita Tower, added in 1979, was the first solar-energy

hotel in the nation.

Today more than 60 shops, many owned by Disney, provide goods and services so that guests need not leave the property during conventions or business meetings for necessities or comforts. There is a sundry store, seamstress, post office, notary public, interpreter, photographer, and babysitter. The hotel was one of the first in the industry to encourage bringing the whole family along on business trips. It offers a Youth Club for children ages 4 to 12 where youngsters are fed and entertained under the supervision of experienced hotel activities counselors.

Disneyland Hotel's full-service Travelport serves as a focal point for locals as well as hotel guests who need airport transportation, demonstrating the key role that the establishment has played in the development of the community. In return the hotel certainly has been influenced by the community's changes.

Michael Bullis, vice-president and general manager since 1982, sees this synergy as ongoing. "Orange County is becoming a travel destination in itself," he says. "Anaheim's convention market will continue to grow, as will Disneyland Park's business. For the hotel to grow and still re-

tain its leading position, we will continue to take bold new steps. We will challenge our existing standards and enhance our facilities to keep meeting the changing needs of our customers successfully."

Bullis notes two major areas that have kept Disneyland Hotel's occupancy levels consistently above the industry average: management's insistence from the beginning on maintaining a level of quality equal to the Disney name, and the founders' entertainment expertise, which encouraged the resort's special attractions to flourish.

New in-room amenities and refurbished guest rooms, halls, and meeting rooms highlight a current multimillion-dollar capital investment program, and possible future expansion is once again under consideration.

Disneyland Hotel was owned and operated by Wrather Corporation, which Jack Wrather formed in 1956. Today the Walt Disney Company owns and operates Disneyland Hotel; the famous Queen Mary luxury liner, now permanently docked in Long Beach as an elegant hotel; and the nearby Spruce Goose, Howard Hughes' legendary flying boat. The dream of these two visionaries, Jack Wrather and Walt Disney, continues.

HYATT REGENCY ALICANTE HOTEL

At the corner of Chapman Avenue and Harbor Boulevard in Garden Grove rises the Hyatt Regency Alicante Hotel, inspired by the famous Spanish resort of the same name.

It's easy to spot the striking luxury hotel and office building complex that soars above a sea of low-rise structures in Garden Grove. Alicante Plaza, with its distinctive 17-story Hyatt Regency Alicante Hotel and adjoining 10-story office tower, makes a bold statement as one of the newest landmarks on Orange County's skyline.

Open since June 1986, the Mediterranean-themed Hyatt Regency Alicante was inspired by the famous Spanish resort of the same name. The complex, enhanced by palm trees and fountains in which giant statues of flamingos dwell, is a surprise and delight to visitors who come to the area for business, conventions, or leisure.

The Hyatt Regency Alicante Hotel and office tower, in postmodern architectural style, are peach-colored with white accents. The plaza sits on 17.7 acres of land within Garden Grove's redevelopment district at the corner of Harbor Boulevard and Chapman Avenue, about one mile from Disneyland and the Anaheim Convention Center. This is the first phase of a mixed-use development that will cover 40 acres and constitute an estimated $300-million investment.

The unusual pair, an $88-million undertaking, is joined by a handsome 160-foot-high glass atrium. This is the first adjoining hotel/office complex of its type in the county.

Several major influences have helped give the plaza its identity. The 400-room Hyatt Regency Alicante Hotel is operated by Hyatt Hotels Corporation, noted as a leading innovator in the hospitality industry. The organization is headquartered in Chicago and has more than 90 hotels in the continental United States, with 18 in California, 10 of which are in Southern California.

Cuisine at the Hyatt Regency Alicante is also a major influence. Featuring the Cafe Alicante, located in the open atrium, the hotel offers guests breakfast, lunch, and dinner in the traditional American style, as well as a spectacular Sunday brunch. The newest addition to the hotel is Papa Geppeto's, a family-style Italian restaurant where guests can choose from a wide range of foods, including exotic pizzas, delicate Veal Francesco, and delicious fresh pastas.

Local ownership also influences the Alicante Plaza's hotel and office tower. Dr. Robert Beauchamp, the well-known Newport Beach dentist and real estate developer, owns the property through Beauchamp Enterprises.

The Hyatt Regency Alicante's management philosophy is simple, according to hotel general manager Jerry Lewin: ". . . to bring in new customers while keeping current customers by offering consistent outstanding friendly service that complements our beautiful facility."

The plaza's very location is an influence, its owners believe. Near five freeways, it faces the important Harbor Boulevard corridor, which borders Disneyland yet is just outside the high-activity area of the amusement park and convention center, offering convenience with tranquility.

The Atrium brings the outside in.
Photo by Jim Mendenhall

Romantic waterfront dining in Newport Beach. Photo by Yana Bridle

PATRONS

The following individuals, companies, and organizations have made a valuable commitment to the quality of this publication. Windsor Publications and the Orange County Chamber of Commerce gratefully acknowledge their participation in *Orange County: An Economic Celebration.*

Allergan, Inc.*
Anaheim Memorial Hospital*
Babcock, Inc.
BFM Aerospace Corporation
Mr. & Mrs. Darryl Dean Booker
Bud's Floors & Interiors
Calcomp Inc.*
California Angels*
Ciba-Geigy Corporation*
Coldwell Banker Commercial
    Real Estate Services
Connector Technology, Inc.*
Coto de Caza*

Deloitte Haskins & Sells*
Disneyland Hotel*
Dow Corning S.T.I.
Emulex*
Ernst & Whinney*
Exterminetics of Southern
    California, Inc.
First American Title Insurance
    Company*
Fluidmaster, Inc.*
Ford Aerospace Aeronutronic
    Division*
Gateway Computer*
Great American First Savings
    Bank
Grubb & Ellis Company
Hoag Memorial Hospital
    Presbyterian*
Hyatt Regency Alicante Hotel*
Fred. S. James & Co. of
    California, Inc.*
Kimberly-Clark Corporation*
Martin Luther Hospital*

Officecom, Inc.
Orange County Fair and
    Exposition Center
Orange County Federal Credit
    Union
Pagers Plus
PCM (Professional Community
    Management)*
C.J. Segerstrom & Sons*
Shiley Incorporated*
Solmar Corporation*
Kathryn G. Thompson
The Tishman West Management
    Corporation/The City*
Unisys Corporation*
United Way of Orange County*

*Partners in Progress of *Orange County: An Economic Celebration.* The stories of these companies and organizations appear in chapters 7-11, beginning on page 128.

ABBREVIATIONS

AM—*Atlantic Monthly*
BOC—*Building Orange County*
EX—*The Executive*
LSC—*Liberty Street Chronicle*
LAT—*Los Angeles Times*
MG—*MetroGuide*
OCB—*Orange County Businessweek*
OCR—*Orange County Register*
PSA—*PSA Magazine*
SCM—*South Coast Metro*

Situated on the hills of Big Canyon, these plush homes surround the Big Canyon Country Club's golf course in Newport Beach. Photo by Michele Burgess

BIBLIOGRAPHY

Personal interviews.

Publications:

Anaheim-Santa Ana Metropolitan Statistical Area. Santa Ana: State of California, Employment Development Department, Employment Data & Research, 1986-87.

Baldassare, Mark. *Orange County Annual Survey*. Irvine: University of California, Public Policy Research Organization, December 1984, 1985, 1986.

Berkman, Leslie. "The Japanese in Orange County." *Los Angeles Times*. Los Angeles: Times-Mirror, April 19, 1987.

Bradbury, Ray. *Orange County*. Toronto: Boulton Publishing Services, 1985.

Brody, Jeffrey. "Little Saigon: County's Vietnamese Enclave Succeeds the American Way." *Orange County Register*. Santa Ana: Freedom Newspapers, January 11, 1987.

Brower, Martin. "Orange County is Tomorrow." *PSA Magazine*. Los Angeles: East/West Network, November 1985.

———. "A Strong and Diverse Economy." Orange County International/Special Report. *The Executive*. Los Angeles: Executive Publications: April 1986.

———. "Temporary Help Firms Flock to Orange County as Service Industries Grow, Demand Rises." *Orange County Report*, Vol. 2, No. 9. Newport Beach: Orange County Report, September 1986.

———. "Orange County III." *PSA Magazine*. Los Angeles: East/West Network, November 1986.

Building Orange County. Santa Ana: Building Industry Association of Southern California/Orange County Region, January/February 1987.

Cabiglio, Josie. "The Mother Teresa of Hart Park." Community Edition. *Orange County Register*. Santa Ana: Freedom News-

papers, March 24, 1987.

Church, George J. "The Boom Towns." *Time*. New York: Time, Inc., June 15, 1987.

Curtis, Cathy. "Time is Right for Expansion at the Newport Art Museum." *Orange County Register*. Santa Ana: Freedom Newspapers, March 22, 1987.

Davis, Andi. "Orange County, USA." Orange County International/Special Report. *The Executive*. Los Angeles: Executive Publications, April 1986.

Dean, Jim. "Greater Orange County MetroGuide." Northridge, California: Windsor Publications, 1984.

DeWolfe, Evelyn. "Orange Business Center Begun." *Los Angeles Times*. Los Angeles: Times-Mirror, May 31, 1987.

Doti, James L. *Chapman College Economic & Business Review*. Orange: Chapman College Center for Economic Research, December 1986.

Economic Development Opportunities for Indochinese Refugees in Orange County. Source: Vietnamese Chamber of Commerce of Orange County, Garden Grove, December 1986.

Evans, Heidi. "Old-timers Heading to Vegas in the Long Run." *Los Angeles Times*. Los Angeles: Times-Mirror, February 1, 1987.

Feibus, Michael. "Strong Growth Predicted in County for Next 15 Years." *Los Angeles Times*. Los Angeles: Times-Mirror, July 31, 1986.

Flamm, Don. "Local Advertising Agencies Move Up in World." *Orange County Businessweek*. Irvine: Orange County Businessweek, August 3, 1987.

Galante, Mary Ann. "18 Lawyers Quit Big County Firm, Set Up Shop in Irvine." *Los Angeles Times*. Los Angeles: Times-Mirror, April 28, 1987.

———. "Legal Boom Brings Pain with Growth." *Los Angeles*

Times. Los Angeles: Times-Mirror, June 21, 1987.

Graebner, Janet E. "Orange County's Penny Dilemma." *California Business*. Los Angeles: California Business News, May 1984.

———. "Riding High on Technology into the 21st Century." *Christian Science Monitor*. Boston: Christian Science Publishing Society, September 24, 1984.

———. "Orange County: Will High Tech Open New Doors?" *California Business*. Los Angeles: California Business News, December 1984.

———. "South Coast Metro." *The Executive*. Los Angeles: Executive Publications, April 1985.

———. "Centennial Planning Under Way." *Orange County Businessweek*. Irvine: Orange County Businessweek, September 29, 1986.

———. "Orange County Performing Arts Center: A World-class Legacy of Private Enterprise." *The Executive*. Los Angeles: Executive Publications, October 1986.

Granelli, James S. "Hometown Brokers Find Their Niche." *Los Angeles Times*. Los Angeles: Times-Mirror, June 7, 1987.

Haas, Jane Glenn. "Builders Ready to Counterattack." *Orange County Register*. Freedom Newspapers, October 7, 1987.

———. "Developers Must Help Solve Road Woes, Lyon Says." *Orange County Register*. Freedom Newspapers, January 7, 1987.

———. "Santa Ana Paving Way for $600 Million 'Urban Village.'" *Orange County Register*. Santa Ana: Freedom Newspapers, January 21, 1987.

Hallan-Gibson, Pamela. *The Golden Promise: An Illustrated History of Orange County*. Northridge, California: Windsor Publications, 1986.

Haney, Fred M. "OC's Venture Capital Community Thriving."

Orange County Businessweek. Irvine: Orange County Businessweek, July 27, 1987.

Hardesty, Greg. "OC Economy to Grow, but Anemic Expansion will Hurt Some Sectors." *Orange County Businessweek.* Irvine: Orange County Businessweek, January 12, 1987.

———. "Dinner Theaters Flourish in County." *Orange County Businessweek.* Irvine: Orange County Businessweek, January 19, 1987.

———. "Hispanic Ads Mean *Bueno* Biz for Firms." *Orange County Businessweek.* Irvine: Orange County Businessweek, August 3, 1987.

Horizon. "Orange County." USArts/Strategies for the 80s. Tuscaloosa, Alabama: Horizon Publishing, January/February 1987.

Jackel, Jonathan. "Bank's New Unit to Shoot for Pacific Rim." *Orange County Businessweek.* Irvine: Orange County Businessweek, February 16, 1987.

James, Rosemary. "Orange County Dynamics in Action." Orange County International/Special Report. *The Executive.* Los Angeles: Executive Publications, April 1987.

Johnson, Pete. "Inside UCI." *Orange Coast Magazine.* Costa Mesa: O.C.N.L., April 1985.

———. "Dead End: The Future Shock of Orange County's Roadways." *Orange Coast Magazine.* Costa Mesa: O.C.N.L., January 1987.

Leinberger, Christopher B. and Charles Lockwood. "How Business is Reshaping America." *The Atlantic Monthly.* Boston: Atlantic Monthly Company, October 1986.

Lesher, Dave. "Slow-growth Forces Lose: Supervisors OK Road Deal." *Los Angeles Times.* Los Angeles: Times-Mirror, October 22, 1987.

Lingle, Arthur J. "Orange County Freeways: Breaking the Bottleneck." *The Executive.* Los Angeles: Executive Publications, September 1986.

Lobdell, William. "Lynn Livingston:

President of Orange County's Largest—and Perhaps Most Entrepreneurial—Advertising Agency Talks About His Company and Profession." *South Coast Metro.* Costa Mesa: Metropolitan Journals, May 1987.

Los Angeles Times. "Growth Debate is Healthy." Editorial. Los Angeles: Times-Mirror, February 22, 1987.

———. "Orange County at Work." Special Report. Los Angeles: Times-Mirror, May 3, 1987.

———. "War and Peace." Editorial. Los Angeles: Times-Mirror, July 23, 1987.

———. "Hospital Will Dedicate its New Cancer Center." Orange County Digest. Los Angeles: Times-Mirror, September 6, 1987.

Menning, Susan. "Socks Alive! It's Cochrane Chase." *Liberty Street Chronicle.* Irvine: Liberty Street Chronicle, April 1984.

Muir, Frederick M. *Los Angeles Times.* Orange County Economic Report. Los Angeles: Times-Mirror, December 28, 1986.

———. "At Work." *Los Angeles Times.* Special Report. Los Angeles: Times-Mirror, May 3, 1987.

McLellan, Dennis. "Orange County Gets a Shot at 'Fame.'" *Los Angeles Times.* Los Angeles: Times-Mirror, March 19, 1987.

Morgan, Judith and Neil. "Orange, A Most California County." *National Geographic.* Volume 159, No.12. Washington, D.C.: National Geographic Society, December 1981.

Mouchard, André. "Spectrum Absorbing Bulk of Area's Industrial Leases." *Orange County Businessweek.* Irvine: Orange County Businessweek, June 22, 1987.

Newton, Edmund. "'Urban Villages' Viewed as Successors to Cities." *Los Angeles Times.* Los Angeles: Times-Mirror, April 16, 1987.

Orange County Businessweek. Largest Accounting Firms in Orange County. Irvine: Orange County Businessweek, January 26, 1987.

Orange County Progress Report. Vol. 23. Santa Ana: County Administrative Office, 1986-87.

Orange County Register. "Orange County: At the Cutting Edge of Tomorrow." The Blue Book. Santa Ana: Orange County Register MetroGroup, 1984.

———. "Growing Pains." Special Report. Santa Ana: Freedom Newspapers, November 23, 1986.

———. "Getting Nowhere Fast." Special Report. Santa Ana: Freedom Newspapers, November 30, 1986.

———. Orange County Focus/Top Ad Agencies. Santa Ana: Freedom Newspapers, February 15, 1987.

———. "Orange County's Image." Special Report. Santa Ana: Freedom Newspapers, June 28, 29, 30, 1987.

Reyes, David. "Hispanic Chamber of Commerce is Formed." *Los Angeles Times.* Los Angeles: Times-Mirror, June 10, 1987.

Robbins, Gary. "UCI's Peltason Sets High Goals, Gets High Praise." *Orange County Register.* Santa Ana: Freedom Newspapers, March 15, 1987.

Rowe, Jeff. "As Competition Grows, More Employers Using Temporary Workers." *Los Angeles Times.* Los Angeles: Times-Mirror, July 7, 1987.

Sanchez, Leonel. "She Gives Food, and Heart, to Park's Homeless." *Los Angeles Times.* Los Angeles: Times-Mirror, March 3, 1987.

Seidenbaum, Art. Book Review/Endpapers. Costa Mesa. *Los Angeles Times.* Los Angeles: Times-Mirror, [November 1983].

Self, Thomas M. "The Challenge of International Trade." Orange County International/Special Report. *The Executive.* Los Angeles: Executive Publications, April 1986.

Simon, Richard V. "UC Irvine." *The Executive.* Los Angeles: Executive Publications, February 1986.

Smith, Chalon. "High-Tech Firm Nurtures Acting Bug." *Los Angeles Times.* Los Angeles: Times-Mirror, March 20, 1987.

Stroud, Ruth. "Asian Banks Try to Widen Appeal." *Orange County Register.* Santa Ana: Freedom Newspapers, January 19, 1986.

———. "The Selling of Orange County." *Orange County Register*. Santa Ana: Freedom Newspapers, April 19, 1987.

Taylor, Cathy. "OC's Long-term Growth Should Outpace State's." *Orange County Register*. Santa Ana, California: Freedom Newspapers, July 30, 1986.

——— and Jonathan Lansner. "How Healthy are Orange County's Banks?" *Orange County Register*. Santa Ana: Freedom Newspapers, March 29, 1987.

Thompson, Kathryn G. "Controlled Growth is Best Answer to Congested Traffic." *South Coast Metro*. Costa Mesa: Metropolitan Journals, October 1987.

Trippett, Frank. "Orange Riviera." *Time*. New York: Time, Inc., August 18, 1986.

Vanderknyff, Rick. "SCR Acting Class Puts Life in Old Dreams." *Los Angeles Times*. Los Angeles: Times-Mirror, February 26, 1987.

———. "New Gallery Puts Art in Focus with Antiques." *Los Angeles*. Los Angeles: Times-Mirror, March 16, 1987.

Vida, Herbert J. Orange County Digest. *Los Angeles Times*. Los Angeles: Times-Mirror, March 22, 1987.

Vranizan, Michelle. "Electronics Firms Told to Plug into Togetherness." *Orange County Businessweek*. Irvine: Orange County Businessweek, January 26, 1987.

———. "Investors Turn to Med-Tech Industry." *Orange County Businessweek*. Irvine: Orange County Businessweek, July 27, 1987.

Weglarz, Nilda. "Ignoring 'Retirement' Age Limit." *Orange County Register*. Santa Ana: Freedom Newspapers, February 2, 1987.

Wong, Herman. "Museum is Offered a Challenge." *Los Angeles Times*. Los Angeles: Times-Mirror, February 28, 1987.

———. "Stage Career Blooms in Hometown Setting." *Los Angeles Times*. Los Angeles: Times-Mirror, December 24, 1986.

The Westin Hotel, located in the South Coast Plaza, looms high above the peaceful Noguchi Garden. Planned working environments such as these are unique to Orange County and contribute significantly to its lifestyle. Photo by Jeff Marks

INDEX

189